Software Quality

Engineering

Tales From The Trenches

Og Maciel

Dedication

To my mother, who has taught me how to see the positive in people, to find happiness under all circumstances, gave me unconditional love, attention and all the encouragement I ever needed to pursue my dreams.

Table of Contents

DEDICATION 3

WHY SHOULD YOU GET THIS BOOK? 6

HOW TO READ THIS BOOK 9

INTRODUCTION 10

NOBODY KNOWS WHAT QE IS 18

THE BROKEN MODEL 22

A BETTER MODEL 29

ON QUALITY ASSURANCE 34

ON QUALITY ENGINEERING 40

THE RAT RACE CLAIMS ANOTHER VICTIM 47

THE (HARD) ROAD TO APPRENTICESHIP 55

APPRENTICESHIP PATTERNS 69

SWIM OR SINK 72

LET THEM WHO NEVER CREATED THEIR OWN FRAMEWORK CAST THE FIRST STONE 78

THE REBIRTH OF ROBOTELLO 83

HINDSIGHT IS 20/20 88

NOT ALL OF YOUR TESTS ARE BELONG TO US 93

EVERYBODY TO THE LEFT 102

BE PART OF THE SOLUTION 110

AIN'T NOBODY GOT TIME FOR THAT 120

THE BALANCING ACT 133

ACKNOWLEDGEMENTS.. 141

ABOUT THE AUTHOR 145

Why Should You Get This Book?

First of all, I have to say that I absolutely love what I do and have been doing for a living for the last 11 years of my life! During these 11 years, I have had the pleasure (yes, pleasure) of being tossed around, torn to pieces and thrown at a lot of scary and difficult situations in the world of software testing!

Armed only with a strong desire to learn and excel at my profession, I have seen, heard and gone through a multitude of experiences, challenges, and opportunities. Have I ever been scared shitless or doubted my decision to become a Quality Engineer? Heck yeah! Have I ever felt like the dumbest person in the companies I have worked on? The answer to that question is a resounding "yes!" Have I ever cried? You can bet your bottom dollar I have! But it has been an amazing journey so far, with rewards (and I'm not talking about monetary rewards only) too numerous to count, and plenty of learning opportunities. Let's just say that there has never been a dull moment in these last 11 years and there is nothing that I would trade for all of these experiences.

If you're still reading, and assuming I have no scared you yet, then let me tell you now why you should continue reading. While I can't say that only 11 years of experience makes me an expert about Quality Engineering, I like to think that I have been a good learner and observer through it all. I also have had the good fortune to have worked with and "rubbed elbows" with some amazing people, who perhaps unknowingly or unwillingly, provide me with precious knowledge, wisdom and "windows" into a brand new world for me.

Like a dry sponge, I did my best to absorb from these people all I could.

- How they handled certain situations, especially when caught by surprise or presented with something entirely new.
- How they learned.
- How they organized their tasks and stayed focused.
- How they reacted when faced with challenges, under pressure.
- How they overcame their obstacles and limitations.

With this book, it is my goal to tell you about some of these situations and experiences and how I have turned them into life and career lessons. Hopefully, they help you become a better, more effective and brave professional.

Through these "tales," I also hope to inspire a new generation of Quality Engineers and guide them through some of the challenges that one is bound to come across when starting out on a new career.

Lastly, for those who, like me, have been working in this field: I hope you'll relate to some of my tales, perhaps sharing a laugh or a tear as you remember how you too may have faced a similar situation, and how you (hopefully) overcame it.

How to Read This Book

In my opinion, the best way to read *Software Quality Engineering: Tales From The Trenches*, is to pick a chapter that attracts your curiosity or may be related to a particular area where you may be looking for guidance or more information, and start there! Each "lesson" chapter is designed to be self-contained, so it is completely okay to go straight into the ones that catch your eyes.

This is not to say that you can't or shouldn't read it all from start to finish. I have added a lot of myself into this book, and if you choose to read through the other chapters, the ones not related to lessons learned, you'll see and learn a great deal about my person, my way of seeing things and my way of thinking.

Therefore, without further ado, let's get started!

Introduction

My entry into the world of software testing and automation started pretty much like many of the quality engineers I've met in the course of my career: I was dragged, kicking and screaming, from my comfortable role as a software engineer back in 2008 to spearhead, whether I wanted it or not, the QA team for our start-up company. Looking back on that day more than 11 years later, I can honestly say that even though it wasn't immediately evident to me, this seemingly innocuous role change was the best decision I have ever **not** made in my professional career.

The first challenge I had to overcome was my own misconception about what a Tester did. From my limited understanding of what happened in QA, I incorrectly assumed that there was no coding involved or required. One merely clicked their way effortlessly through a software application's user interface (up until then I had worked on a web-based application that controlled and managed virtual appliances), looking for ways to either "break it" or at least assure that its basic functionality worked as expected. Other than this, there wasn't much guidance as to how the job should be done, what quality really meant and, most importantly, how to ensure it!

The most important expectation for my new role seemed to be:

- don't let any regressions slip into the product in between releases and
- make sure that, whatever issues had been found by our paying customers and were eventually fixed by our developers, were indeed fixed in the next version.

Given that I had no formal training in programming, engineering or testing, and that I was a self-taught software developer, I decided to embrace my own ignorance and immediately started putting together a list of all the web pages that were exposed to our users through our web application. This was followed by another list of all actions and elements that could be interacted with, regardless of whether they were buttons, dropdown lists, radio buttons, text fields or links.

I then wrote down the types of interactions for each of those web elements, for every single web page, and what the expected outcome would be.

Page Name	Web Element	Input Value	Expectations
Login	Text Field	Admin	
	Text Field	Password	
	Button	Click	Login User Admin
Login	Text Field	Admin	
	Text Field	<EMPTY>	
	Button	Click	Error notification about empty password

It was a very rudimentary and incomplete process for sure, one that did not include testing any boundary scenarios (e.g., what should not happen when some unexpected value was plugged into a field?), integration with other external tools, performance or scalability.

In spite of this, it felt like an improvement to the nonexistent process by which we had until then been shipping our product to our customers, and one that at least provided me with a checklist of test cases so that I never forgot to test any given area or feature.

Eventually, and luckily rather quickly for me, it dawned on everyone that as our product became more complex and our support matrix grew more extensive, it would be humanly impossible for anyone, let alone a Team of One, to execute all the identified test cases from my list. There were just too many permutations of web browsers and operating systems. Our users, reasonably so, expected our web application to behave the same way no matter what device they were using.

After a couple of intense days and evenings, where I sat nearly alone at the office to make sure that we shipped a new release by the assigned date, it was clear that I would have to learn how to automate my test cases or I'd go completely insane!

We were pretty much a Python and Linux shop, so choosing Python as the programming language to build a new testing framework was a logical choice. I had a pool of seasoned Python developers around me who could potentially provide me some guidance and bail me out, if necessary, to get something off the ground. Also, since the main focus would be to test the web application portion of our product, I chose a well-known technology, Selenium "a suite of tools to automate web browsers across many platforms."

Now, it is pretty straightforward to read a couple of articles online about how web application testing should be automated, but starting from scratch without a single working example or model of how to do it right is an entirely different story! After two very unsuccessful and frustrating weeks with no significant progress, and right before desperation set in, upper management decided to hire a new person to join the team and help me out. This was someone who already had a few startups under his belt and was well versed on how to bootstrap an automation team for testing software products. His name was Andrew McCabe, and I basically owe him all I have ever learned and know today about software testing!

Under his tutelage, whether he knew that he was mentoring me or even saw me as his pupil or not, my career as a Quality Engineer finally took off. Through the many long hours and weekends that we worked together, side by side, a real baptism by fire you could say, and shepherding half a dozen releases of rBuilder (that's what the product was named), I came to understand a number of things:

- Software Quality Engineering is much more than just pushing buttons, clicking on items and following scripts! It is okay to do that early in your career, but if after a couple of years you're still doing it, you should probably either change your ways or find another job!
- You can be a Developer and spend your entire career only knowing about the parts of an application that you touched, but the same cannot be said about a Quality Engineer worth their salt. Not understanding

how the entire application stack works is not an option!

- Quality will always be more important than quantity! This applies not only to the applications that you test, but also the code that you write and the way you do your job.

- If you don't take pride in what you do, then what is the point of doing it at all?

- Quality is everyone's responsibility! Though I wish it were true, there is no Quality Magic Wand! If you want to produce Quality Products, make sure that it is there from the beginning!

- Testers deserve and should have a seat at the table whenever a product is being planned, designed or implemented! Their opinion matters! If someone attempts to erect a wall to separate Testers from the rest of the Team, Tear. It. Down!

- When you spend an average of 12-15 hours a day, 7 days a week, with a Team of dedicated and passionate people, all working toward the same goal, tension and stress are bound to increase. It is especially important during those moments where friction and anxiety are about to flare up to be able to keep a cool head and stay calm. It is also during these moments that social skills pay off big time, as you must be able to work around whatever obstacles may come up and get things done, on time, as a Team.

- There is no Us or Them. There is only The Team, and if this is not the mentality or the environment you're working in, you don't have a Team!

There were many similar lessons I learned during those fast-paced, crazy years at **rPath Inc.** and looking back today to where I am and what I have accomplished so far, I can honestly say that those were happy days and all the bumps and knocks I experienced only helped me to become a better professional. A "school of hard knocks" of a sort for sure, but I would not trade those 5 1/2 years for anything!

This book is my humble attempt at sharing some of the lessons I have learned from this experience as well as other lessons that came with another 7+ years working in the Quality Engineering Department at **Red Hat Inc.**, my current employer. I honestly feel that many of these lessons are directly responsible for the relative success I have had so far.

I hope that they may be of use to those of you out there fighting the good fight to ensure Software Quality. Even better, to awaken in those of you not yet familiar with this field, the desire to learn more about Quality Engineering, an exciting career where learning something new every single day is the norm. A place where a good day in the office is when you were able to avoid catastrophe by identifying severe and critical issues in the design and usability of the software your company is developing way before it gets placed into a customer's hands. A place where you're not only encouraged to "think outside the box" to design a reliable and robust automated process for testing a customer's scenario, but chances are that there is no box! Like a MacGyver, you'll have to use your brain and whatever else is available around you to achieve your goal!

If after reading this book you decide to take the plunge and perhaps one day join our ranks, then I'll feel that I have done my job, and yours should be about to begin!

Og Maciel, Chapel Hill, NC - October 1st, 2018

Nobody Knows What QE Is

Every time I meet someone new, usually shortly after the initial introductions and small talk that tend to make up these types of situations, and right before it gets to that dreadful uncomfortable, awkward silence, the conversation inevitably turns toward what one does for a living. For me, specifically, this part of the conversion tends to go a little bit like this:

- **New acquaintance**: "So, what do you do Og?"
- **Me**: Well, I'm a Senior Manager for a team of Quality Engineers."
- **New acquaintance**: "Oh, you mean QA?"
- **Me**: "No, QE!"
- **New acquaintance**: "????"
- **Me**: "Sigh"

Unfortunately, the term Quality Engineer (QE) is not as well known or utilized as the terms Quality Assurance (QA), Quality Control (QC) or just plain Tester, and for better or worse, anyone working in the field of software testing ends up eventually being "lumped" into the category of Quality Assurance. One then is said to work in QA or to be a "QA person."

First of all, let me get something off my chest and hopefully make something clear: Quality Assurance, or QA, is **not a profession**. QA **is**, however, a **process** usually used to determine whether a product, be that software or goods or whatever, actually provides a set of features and that they operate and perform as advertised. So while one cannot be a QA, one can assert QA for a living. The term QA seems to be the one that most people associate with testing in general and because of it, it has become the way to describe the title for those who test software or products for a living.

As I mentioned in the introduction, it has been my experience that for most of the time product quality is something not well defined or even seriously considered until much later in the lifecycle of a product, almost as an afterthought. It is only when a company starts feeling the pressure from unhappy paying customers about the (lack of) quality of their product, that the decision is finally made to bootstrap a team responsible for ensuring Quality. Usually, an unfortunate developer is dragged, kicking and screaming-sounds familiar to you?-in protest from their cubicle and entrusted with the dubious honor of starting the QA team. No further instructions as to how precisely this is to be accomplished or how quality is to be quantified is provided.

Another murky item in this business is also the difficulty in adequately defining what quality really means. If your job is to assure that a product has high quality, how do you do that without a clear understanding and team consensus for what quality is?

For instance, is a product with no reported customer complaints a high-quality product? Does a product that provides all advertised features but exhibits many usability issues have better quality than a product that has less working features but zero usability issues for those that do work?

Chances are that if you were to get five different professionals doing QA from different companies (or even departments from the same company) and were to pose the question of what quality is, you'd be fortunate if at least two of them gave you the same or similar answers.

Something else I also noticed is that nobody outside QA knows what really goes on in QA. The general stereotype is that there is some testing, button clicking or lever pulling going on before the product goes out the door, but nobody really seems to know or care at this point about what actually happens behind that door.

Even worse, and this is my biggest pet peeve of all, is the misconception that someone in QA does not write code! It is generally assumed that those on QA basically spend all of their working hours following a script that someone else wrote for them, detailing which buttons to push, what to input into a field and what to expect of the product when a particular action is executed.

Needless to say, the stereotype is also that all of these interactions are manually performed by someone. If they so happen to have a suite of automated tests that can be executed to remove the repetitiveness out of these tasks, it is assumed that the tests must have been designed and written by a software developer, since "people in QA don't really write code."

Grrr, this one really yanks my chain! Is it any wonder that people get a confused look on their faces when they hear the words "Quality" and "Engineering" put together? "How can someone be an engineer if all they do is click buttons?" one may ask.

I'd like now to take a quick detour and talk about some other factors that, in my opinion, have also contributed to not only generating more confusion but, also portray this profession in such a way as to make it look useless, inefficient, and counterproductive to the future and progress of a company. Seems pretty daunting and discouraging, doesn't it? Well, hang in there as I explain.

The Broken Model

To this day, the process by which many software companies take a piece of software (i.e., The Product) from its original idea to the point where it is available for purchase or for use by customers, follows the traditional waterfall model for software engineering.

Wikipedia has the following to say about it:

> *"The waterfall model is a relatively linear sequential design approach for certain areas of engineering design. In software development, it tends to be among the less iterative and flexible approaches, as progress flows in largely one direction ("downwards" like a waterfall) through the phases of conception, initiation, analysis, design, construction, testing, deployment and maintenance."*

One of the key elements from this description, which I strongly feel is noteworthy and needs to be expanded, is the fact that making changes to the product becomes linearly harder (or more expensive in terms of time, effort and actual monetary costs) to execute as it gets closer and closer to its completion and eventual ship date.

In other words, even if someone finds a flaw in the original design or implementation for how a particular feature of the product is supposed to behave, the team or individuals responsible for getting it out the door and into the hands of waiting customers are faced with the following dilemma:

- Stop the release process, and thus delay the release date (potentially frustrating customers and users) so that the original requirements can be revisited, adjustments can be made to fix the erroneous behavior, and then put the product back on the release train, or
- Keep the release on track and deal with the issue at a later time or just absorb the risk.

The image below further illustrates how the standard waterfall model proposes that "progress flows from the top to the bottom, like a cascading waterfall." As you can see, the Verification phase only happens at the very end of the software lifecycle, when all features are supposed to be completed, and all defects are fixed, right before the product is shipped.

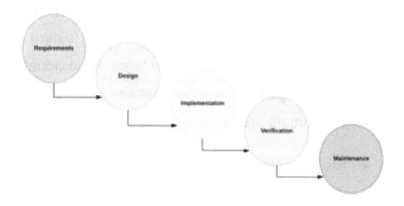

"What are some of the costs or problems inflicted on a product by following this process?", You may ask. Well, allow me to share some of my personal thoughts on this subject based on my own real-world experience in this field.

First and foremost, consider the fact that most of the time, companies want and need to build a sizable and reliable list of customers, willing to pay for their services and products, to keep the companies and their employees... well... employed. Even if we're talking about a startup that has some level of funding from investors and therefore some leeway for not being profitable for a while, this funding is not unlimited, and eventually, the goal is for the company to become independent and create a sustainable business model, which requires getting paying customers.

The first order of business is to identify the market that shows the most promising opportunities for growth (i.e., sales) and is most likely to be receptive to your product.

24

Once this market is clearly identified, the next step is to determine what specific problems your product will either completely solve, improve on, or at least make it more manageable and less of a burden for customers.

Next, some type of feature requirements are put together, usually by one or more Product Managers, and the release process for the product is officially started. This culminates with the handoff of the desired requirements to a team of Developers who are then asked to design and implement what will eventually become the final product.

In the meanwhile, the Program Manager (or Managers) will most likely go back to exploring new growth and business opportunities and start planning requirements for the next version of the product.

When all the design sessions are completed, all the code is written, reviewed and merged, and requirements are fully implemented, there is a formal process by which a "build" is produced and handed off to one or more waiting Testers, initiating the Verification phase. It is during this phase that this "build", once deployed and configured, is used by the Testers to ensure that it provides the expected functionality advertised by the original requirements.

Once this handoff is completed, chances are that the team of Developers will have received a brand new set of requirements from the Program Manager and the Design and Implementation phase is once again started for them, thus keeping the cascading effect flowing down.

So what happens then if a flaw or design issue is found during the Verification phase by one of the Testers? First off, the defect must be reported and discussed with the Development team so that one of the following possible outcomes can be determined:

- Is the product or feature behaving as expected and therefore there is not really an issue?
- If this is the case, could it be that the feature then is not fully understood by the Tester, which led to an erroneous diagnosis?
- If this is the case, is there documentation for the feature in question? Could it be that the documentation is inaccurate or incomplete?
- If the product or feature is not behaving as expected based on the Design phase, could it be that the original requirement was incorrect or incomplete?

Other possible outcomes from this discussion could also be that, yes, a real defect has been found with the product and the team must then decide what to do with it:

- Ignore it (don't laugh, I have seen it happen before)

- Fix it right away
- Ship the product and document the defect as a Known Issue which is not considered a release blocker, with the promise of fixing it "real soon."

Regardless of the final outcome, every time one needs to "swim back up the waterfall," the team responsible for that specific "upstream" phase has already moved on to their next feature or requirement. The knowledge required to address the issue is not as fresh in their minds as it was back when the feature was actually being implemented. You can almost hear the rusty cogs grinding in people's brains as they try to recollect how something was done and what the original design was.

This backward flux will continue to move "upstream" until the information required to make a decision is hopefully reached, and a plan of action is put into place.

The cost for such a typical scenario is that the "machinery" has to be put on hold every time something doesn't go according to plan. The Verification phase stops, perhaps blocked on a critical issue. The Implementation phase is also halted as Developers shift their focus to work with their fellow Testers to determine if there is an issue or not. The Requirements gathering and Design phases may also be impacted if there is no clear guidance on how to proceed with the found problem (Do we fix it? Now? Later?). Worst of all, since Verification only happens toward the end of the process, these types of interruptions can occur multiple times before a product can ever get shipped.

Sadly, it is here that Testers end up unjustifiably getting a bad reputation and may become segregated from the rest of the Team. "Stop finding defects this late in the process," you may hear someone say, or "Why can't you keep up with the Developers?" or, one of my favorites, "Let's just throw some more people at the Verification phase."

Even though I may be exaggerating things a little bit here, I have seen this happen multiple times in many different companies I worked for in the past. Not only is this costly for a company, but it also exerts a heavy toll on every single person involved in the process.

What we need, in my opinion, is a better model!

A Better model

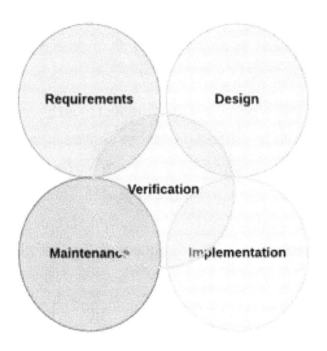

To improve the costly problem of finding defects late in the release process, the most critical change we need to put in place is to shorten the feedback loop between:

- The Verification phase, where most problems are found and identified, and
- The "upstream" phases, where actions and decisions take place with a more direct impact on the flow of the product.

The sooner a problem can be identified in the release process, the sooner remediation measures can be discussed and planned, decisions made and corrective actions executed. This should hopefully help to keep progress for the product through the different phases as close to its original schedule as possible and with minimal effect on its final delivery date.

Even if the release date for a product must be adjusted to accommodate any required changes derived from this early feedback loop, at least the entire Team will be in a condition to make this decision as early as possible. Therefore everyone's expectations can be adjusted according to this decision. This is especially important for the Marketing team, because they must keep expectant customers informed of any delays that may prevent them from getting a highly anticipated new feature, or a fix for a vital defect hindering their use of the product.

Now, it may not be immediately apparent why having a Verification phase during the Requirements and Design phases is so essential, but please bear with me as I explain it.

As a Tester for a product, it is hoped and assumed that with time and experience, a useful collection of knowledge and patterns about how the entire product operates will emerge, ultimately providing someone responsible for the testing of a product with the unique opportunity to become a **Subject Matter Expert** (SME, pronounced smee) for said product.

One advantage of becoming an SME is that you develop a more holistic view about the product so that you, not only understand how all features come together but are also intimately aware of where the pain points and usability issues are for existing customers. This can provide valuable information to Program Managers, such as:

- Should the Team really spend all their energies and resources to add more new shiny features to attract more paying customers - potentially capturing new segments of the market - or
- Should they also allocate some cycles to improve the overall user experience, hence developing the product and making it more stable and user-friendly?

Starting earlier and being present at all phases of the software lifecycle also allows Testers to get started with their own planning and design sessions. This allows them to ensure that they have proper infrastructure, be it hardware for their systems and processes, or changes in their automated testing frameworks, to be prepared to handle the required testing environments and support matrix well in advance.

I don't claim that all Testers have this high level of insight and experience early during their careers. But for those who have been working in this field for a while and continuously seek to improve themselves, this is a very possible outcome, and the value that this type of experience brings to the entire Team should not be wasted or only tapped when the product is being tested at the very end. It is too late by then!

What about the Implementation phase? How can shifting the Verification phase to take place in parallel here provide value? By getting an early peek at the code that will translate all requirements and designs into working features, Testers can then:

- Start asking valuable questions about the code implementation
- Write User Stories and Test Cases to satisfy a feature's requirements
- Confirm that their testing strategy is sufficient to cover the expected behaviors or expose implementation gaps that wouldn't meet those expectations
- Start writing automated tests which can then be executed side by side with any code changes Developers commit, so that failures are quickly caught, identified and fixed.

A "shift to the left" of the Verification phase, allows Developers and Testers to effectively work with each other, shortening the feedback loop between finding defects and getting them fixed. It can also potentially eliminate the traditional "handoff" step as both code Implementation and Verification phases should be taking place at the same time.

When Developers and Testers collaborate this closely, the level of confidence that the product will work according to its original design requirements is much higher. Testers will no longer be in a position to become the "bad guys," finding defects and problems too late in the process. This is a massive win for the entire Team!

Now that I have covered some of the misconceptions and stereotypes behind Quality Engineering, and explained how a typical waterfall software lifecycle model can be detrimental to a company, I want to compare and contrast Quality Assurance and Quality Engineering before getting started with some of the lessons I have learned while working as a Quality Engineer. I'm confident that once you know what the differences are, you'll agree with me that being a Quality Engineer is the most exciting and challenging path you'll want to take.

On Quality Assurance

According to Wikipedia, Quality Assurance or QA

"is a way of preventing mistakes and defects in manufactured products and avoiding problems when delivering solutions or services to customers."

It is a process by which one or more Testers follow a series of steps and procedures with the single purpose of making sure that a product functions as designed.

In the world of software products, this process usually implies the following workflow:

- The source code developed to implement all planned features is committed to a central code repository
- Unit tests are executed and pass before any code being actually merged
- This source code can then potentially be compiled into some type of artifact (also known as a "build") which can be installed on a system
- This build is then handed off to a team of Testers so that they can start the Verification phase

It is during this last step that the process of Quality Assurance begins. This is where Testers need to ensure that what constitutes the build, meets the expected behavior and functionality according to the original requirements from the Program Manager. However, often times, these requirements may not necessarily cover every single use case.

In my experience, most of the time they may only include what is referred to as a "happy path," supposed to represent the most common actions and behaviors that the end users may perform while using the product. The main idea is that, as long as the customer uses the product exactly as described by the "happy path," and as long as Testers can certify that the product at least supports that workflow, nothing should then prevent the product from being shipped.

When there aren't any requirements at all, a sad but prevalent case, it is then up to the Testers to figure out how to best exercise the new functionality. Now, remember how the waterfall model for software development puts QA at the very end of the process? This particular scenario can be further complicated if the Testers are seeing the product or new features for the first time.

By this point, the clock is already ticking, and the Marketing team is eager to send out press releases and let the customers know that the highly touted product is available. There is not a lot of time left for Testers to properly learn about the product, or for the design of complex testing strategies, nor their implementation or execution.

One could say that covering the "happy path" is definitely better than not covering anything at all. However, it is regrettable that what separates our customers from just good enough to a high-level quality product is the fact that the Verification phase is often rushed, and those "responsible" for validating it and ensuring its quality are testing a completely unknown, fast-moving black box.

So what is a team of Testers to do? You roll with the punches and do your best to come up with one or more "happy path" tests, just to make sure that the most basic functionality of the product is exercised. I guess one could also pray that the end users won't deviate too much from everyone's assumptions of how the customers will use the product, but I wouldn't recommend that solution.

If any regressions or new defects are found during the Verification phase, depending on how many days are left before the release date (also known as the GA date), that is when things can get really interesting for the entire Team since a decision must be made:

- Do you fix the regression or new defect, or

- Do you keep moving forward to the scheduled release date?

It is during these situations that those doing QA are given the dubious honor of becoming the "Release Gatekeepers." Urgent meetings are quickly scheduled, and all eyes and attention from all stakeholders are heavily shifted to the Testers group, as the dreadful question is uttered: "Do we have the green light from QA to proceed or do we need to delay the release?"

As a Tester, if you don't have a clear understanding of how a regression or newly found defect in the product will affect the final customer, when you cannot quantify the impact that releasing the product with a known issue will have on the customers, how can you then provide a concrete answer? Trust me, it is not a comfortable position or desired situation to be in.

When all you do as a Tester is QA, you're always reacting to whatever comes your way, and one can only handle so many surprises and put out so many fires before losing one's sanity. If a new build lands on your plate, you drop what you're working on, install it and start the validation process. If something fails during this process, you stop and investigate. If a new feature is added, you scramble to learn about it as quickly as possible.

So in my opinion, in many ways working on QA is akin to being like Superman. Yes, I am referring to the Man of Steel, the Superman from comics and movies, which doesn't sound too bad, right? I mean, who doesn't want to be compared to a superhero? Superman is an incredibly powerful being who can fly, has super strength, x-ray vision and is supposed to be faster than a bullet.

If you've ever read the old Superman comics or watched the old tv series and movies, the way that he solves problems usually goes like this:

- Superman is flying around, minding his own business when, all of a sudden, due to his super abilities, he hears or sees someone in desperate need for help, or
- A plane is falling from the sky, or
- Someone is tied up to the train tracks as a bullet train is fast approaching

What does he do? He takes advantage of his super speed to arrive at the "crime scene" in the nick of time. He then either safely carries the entire plane down to safety or, stops the moving train before it can reach the unfortunate victim (why he never chose to untie the victim and let the train go through without destroying it is something I never really understood).

Thinking on your feet, reacting very quickly without a lot of time to think and using your brain and brawn, isn't that a lot like what one does when doing QA?

In my opinion, doing QA is precisely like being Superman!

On Quality Engineering

When I was still learning about Quality Assurance and test automation early in my career, I had a pretty well-established routine for a while. I was always the first person to arrive at the office before 08:00 AM and the first thing I did was to make a fresh pot of coffee (back then we used to order Counter Culture coffee). While that was brewing, I would then proceed to my desk, plug my laptop to the docking station, and make sure that my sessions were successfully restored precisely the same way I had left them the night before. Even though it was already 2008 and Linux had made a lot of progress, the fact that things such as docking and undocking a laptop just worked was something I was still getting used to.

Once I had gotten a tall mug of coffee, the next order of business was to take a look at the results from our nightly automated pipeline and check if all of our tests had successfully passed. Note that I did not say "check if they had executed" but "if they had passed."

Our release process was so robust and reliable that I never had to worry if a nightly build had been generated with all the code changes from the previous day. This is something that I was able to take for granted, and I could dedicate all of my focus instead on the automation part of my job.

Anyone who has experienced the unreliability of a flaky build system can probably relate to the sense of frustration and hopelessness that one encounters when you arrive at work expecting to see the results of your hard work to then find out that due to a failed compilation procedure, your tests were never executed.

Side Story

Earlier in my career at rPath, we had 5 different lava lamps connected to our build system, each one representing one of the various components which together made up our main product. As our team of developers reviewed and committed code to the central code repository, a series of jobs were automatically started which at a minimum triggered the execution of the Unit tests for that product. If the newly committed code happened to break the test suite, the lava lamp corresponding to that product would turn on, and everyone would immediately see that someone had "broken" the product. If all lava lamps were turned on at the same time, then a hockey siren with throbbing lights would then go off, lighting up the entire engineering area. It may sound harsh but it worked really well, and if I remember correctly, I only saw that siren go off twice in all the time that we used those lava lamps.

As I reviewed the results of our functional test suite, assuming that none of our tests had failed, I could then take a look at our issue tracking system to see what tasks had been assigned to me for that week. However, If one or more tests had failed, then I'd then start looking at the generated logs to figure out if our tests had uncovered a regression in the last build.

Usually, that would require that I create a new defect report in our defects tracking system. If my investigation showed that the real culprit was a poorly designed test, I'd then create a task for myself to review its logic and fix the problem later in the day.

Around 10:00 AM all of our engineers would have arrived (I'd be on my second cup of coffee by then), and we'd all stand up in the middle of the engineering area in a circle, and start our daily status meeting. The rules for it were straightforward:

- Tell everyone what you are planning to work on

- Inform if you're blocked on anything or anyone (which would then lead to a separate conversation with the Program Manager and whoever else was needed to unblock the situation)
- Do it all in only a couple of minutes

No matter how big we ever got (at a point we had approximately 30 engineers), getting through our daily standup status meeting on time was something we never messed with and it was never skipped. If one of the more senior people were not around, someone would kick it off, and before I could finish that second cup of coffee, the meeting was over, and everyone had a clear plan of action for the day.

Another benefit from this daily ritual which I learned to appreciate was the fact that it was virtually impossible for anyone not to know what the entire team was working on or what the priorities were. When the whole team knew who was responsible for what and who was blocking you from completing your tasks, it was easy to communicate and collaborate with your fellow engineer. It also helps to avoid a lot of problems that arise when people don't interact well or don't have full visibility into what people are doing.

Additionally, if anyone happened to take a day off (due to a planned vacation or sick day, for example), any one of the other engineers could step in, take over where that person had left off, and work on their task almost as if they had been working on it all along. Communication and transparency were crucial to our success, and I feel that we did that really well.

So, what is the definition of a Quality Engineer then? Once again I will turn to our friends at Wikipedia, who have the following to say about this topic:

"Quality engineering is the discipline of engineering that creates and implements strategies for quality assurance in product development and production as well as software development."

The article also mentions an impressive list of "body of knowledge" that someone in this profession should have and exert as part of their role, such as (to name a few):

- Management and leadership
- Product and process design
- Reliability and maintainability
- Continuous improvement
- Quality management and planning tools
- Continuous improvement techniques
- Preventive action
- Risk management

Wow, that is quite an impressive list and looking back to those early days, I can't help but draw many parallels between what-in my opinion-a Quality Engineer must do and the skills I picked up while working there.

Leadership? Yes. At any given day anyone could pick up the reins, crack the whip, and get folks moving in the right direction. Process design and continuous improvement? We were so ahead of our time that we had no choice but to be creative and solve issues that no one else was even dreaming of doing. Being proactive about possible problems, building new tools and technologies and assessing risks and how to address or at least mitigate them? Once again, we did it all.

But anyhow, that was Wikipedia's definition. If you want my personal definition of what a Quality Engineer is, then my short and perhaps over-simplified answer is: **Quality Engineers are like Batman**! Here's why:

Contrary to doing only Quality Assurance (i.e., being Superman) and being on the receiving end of the software lifecycle, a Quality Engineer (much like Batman) must prepare himself by:

- Building a vast base of knowledge about a multitude of subjects
- Learn new skills and techniques

- Plan, design and implement systems and tools

You don't think that the Batcave was fully furnished or that the utility belt was handed off to Bruce Wayne overnight, did you? I'm sure that his fortune made things a bit easier but I'm also confident that it took a lot of his time and dedication to get to where he became efficient and good at what he did.

What did Kal-El (Superman's birth name) ever do to become Superman? Nothing. Once he left his home planet of Krypton and was exposed to our solar system's yellow Sun, he immediately acquired his superpowers.

When Batman, er, a Quality Engineer needs to solve a problem, he or she must perform detailed and extensive research, gather as many data points and facts as possible, and use logic and intuition (no gut feelings here) to reach a working solution. When everything else fails, a Quality Engineer will become resourceful and use whatever is available to resolve the problem.

Yup, being a Quality Engineer is like being Batman!

The Rat Race Claims Another Victim

The year 2006 was a significant mark in my career: for the second time since I graduated from college and started working professionally, I found myself unemployed. Whereas when the first time this happened I left of my own accord and only had a small child, this time around my project had been terminated (I was working as a consultant in NYC) and my wife and I were both expecting our second child.

Having spent the bulk of my years living in Northern New Jersey, I quickly realized the perils of not having a job and having to support, with the help of my wife, our growing family. Everything is astronomically expensive in that area, and even with the salary of my wife, we knew that we would not be able to survive for too long.

That was in the hot days of July and even though we were relying pretty heavily on our savings, for some reason I was still blissfully optimistic about my chances of finding a high paying job that would allow me to maintain my living style and pay for the two bedroom apartment we had in Fort Lee, New Jersey.

I say "blissfully optimistic" because had I learned from my previous experience, I would have remembered that nobody seems to hire around the hot summer days. Just like the school year in the United States begins in September, it appears that hiring also follows the same pattern, or at least that is how I felt.

Every morning I'd start bright and early and would begin my job search. I looked through the local newspapers, job websites and called some friends from previous jobs to see if anyone had any leads for me.

I also came up with the theory that sending emails to potential hiring managers during the afternoon hours was not a good idea. I felt that the hours after lunch would not be as productive to anyone whose job was to parse through (probably) dozens of resumes every day. In my mind, nothing would be more tedious than trying to match what people wrote down as being their interests and skillsets to whatever position they were trying to fill.

So once I had culled enough interesting positions that matched my interests, my afternoons were spent on preparing all the emails and different versions of my resume to look more attractive and better fit with their desired requirements. Before "signing off" for the day, usually after 6 pm, I then sent all of my emails and hoped for some replies.

As the days wore on and my savings slowly started to dwindle, so did my optimism and patience. Even though I did get an occasional reply from someone interested in chatting with me, I could not get past the first interview round. After a few weeks of rejections, I was willing to take any job whatsoever, anything that would allow me to pay for my bills and help me avoid the looming end of the road.

I remember one day when, after studying and preparing myself for an important interview for a position within a bank as a C# developer, I fell asleep sometime after 3 am and woke up 4 hours later when my wife found me with my head buried under a couple of technical books.

I took a quick shower, got dressed and drove to my interview, mustering as much courage and enthusiasm as I could, to try to land a job that I was not really interested in taking. After talking to the existing three developers and getting a sense for what the environment was like, my would-be manager led me to a secluded room where I then had to take a coding test.

I don't know what happened, but as soon as I took a look at the first problem, how to create a connection to an existing SQL Server instance using ADO.NET, my mind went completely blank! I could not remember what to do, and at the end of the 40 minutes allocated to this task, I had answered just the first problem. I never heard back from the bank.

After a few more rejections and some sleepless nights of mind storming and planning with my wife, we both decided that what we needed was a new place to live.

Back then, my younger sister was still pursuing her Master's degree at the University of North Carolina at Chapel Hill. Since I had already visited the town and very much enjoyed the area, its people and the laid-back atmosphere (compared to the "rat race" of living close to NYC), I threw some clothes in my suitcase, packed my old but reliable laptop and bought a single round-trip airplane ticket to North Carolina.

I landed at the Raleigh-Durham International airport in the middle of September and went immediately to work on scouting job opportunities. Due to the many universities and technology-related companies in the area, I pretty soon found quite a few promising job leads, including a role as a developer for an oncology department at Duke University.

I believe that my degree in Biochemistry and previous experience working for two pharmaceutical companies as a software developer looked interesting enough to them, as I received an invitation for a job interview the very next day after emailing them my resume.

Being physically in North Carolina and having a local address (I used my sister's) was vital to getting people to respond to my job inquiries too since I highly doubt that anyone would be willing to talk to me if they knew that I lived in New Jersey. By that weekend I had already had a few interviews and managed to line up a few more for the following week, including one in New Jersey, probably still from my earlier job search.

I did the New Jersey-to-North Carolina back and forth dance for two weeks, going home on weekends to see my wife and daughter. Despite my efforts and the interviews I went through, I just couldn't find anyone willing to hire me. Something seemed to be missing, and I couldn't tell what it was.

Turns out that "Lady Luck" was right around the corner and all that it was required of me was to attend two free events that were happening on the same day.

Remember how I mentioned that my sister was studying at the University of North Carolina? Well, on a Thursday morning, right before she went to her classes, we made a deal: I'd attend a poetry reading session with her that afternoon if she would attend a local Linux User Group (LUG) hosted at Red Hat's old headquarters building on North Carolina State University's Centennial Campus.

That afternoon we both attended the poetry reading session, grabbed a bite to eat at one of the local restaurants and just when we were supposed to drive to Raleigh for the Linux event, my sister changed her mind and told me that she didn't want to go anymore.

I confess that since I was flying back to New Jersey in the early morning the next day, and having had a long day myself, I almost gave in and went back to her apartment. But history seems to be full of these types of occurrences when the tiniest, most mundane decisions often dictate the outcome of many successes and failures. I firmly believe that my history was forever changed when I chose to ignore my tiredness and my sister's reluctance, and chose instead to drive to Raleigh!

To make a long story short, I happened to meet with a fellow Linux enthusiast who knew me from my blog and involvement with the **Ubuntu GNU/Linux** community. We started talking, and when he heard that I was planning to move to the area and was looking for a job, he quickly interrupted me and said: "I have the perfect place for you to apply. You should send them your resume as soon as possible."

The rest of the evening was a blur for me since I couldn't stop thinking about the door that had just opened up. After so many interviews and missed opportunities, did I have the strength to try it one more time or was I ready to return home and accept my failure of not being able to find a new job?

It turns out I still had a bit of energy left. As soon as I got back to my sister's apartment that night, despite the late hour and having to pack for my flight the next day, I sat down for 5 minutes and sent my resume to a **Ken VanDine** who was looking for a Python developer. I think that was around 11 pm.

The very next day I woke up early and decided to check my email one more time before putting the laptop away. Boy was I surprised when I saw a reply to my job application inviting me to "ping" Ken on IRC as soon as possible.

Luckily for me, Ken was an early riser, and I had no difficulty in locating him on the freenode server. We chatted for a few minutes, quickly switching to a phone call that lasted about 30 minutes or so, and by the time we hung up I had a tentative job offer on the table!

The offered salary was 40% less than what I was making before, but if I were to accept it, it would allow me to realize a personal dream: work with open source tools and run GNU/Linux on my work computer all the time!

I told Ken that I was going to think about the offer over the weekend and talk it over with my wife before giving my final answer, but who was I kidding? Despite the significant salary cut, I felt that this was a fantastic opportunity that I could not afford to pass on.

What followed was an intense week of packing, saying goodbye to our parents, and friends and a 500 miles trip to our new home in Chapel Hill.

Little did I know that the most turbulent days of my professional career were about to begin.

The (Hard) Road to Apprenticeship

Hitting Rock Bottom

My first job working for a company that used open source software to build their products started on October 2nd, 2006 when I joined a young startup called rPath, located in the outskirts of Raleigh, North Carolina.

Everything that happened for the first couple of days was entirely novelty to me.

- They handed me a brand new laptop that I could use however I saw fit.
- They allowed me to install whatever distribution of GNU/Linux I chose, even though they had two distributions they maintained in-house.
- There were FREE snacks, drinks, and GOOD coffee in the breakroom. Providing employees with these things may be the norm nowadays, but while working for the State of New York as a consultant, the only thing we had that was free was water from the water cooler. If you wanted to get some coffee, you had

better go outside and buy your cup of diluted coffee from a street vendor!

- People were friendly and very welcoming. Again, keep in mind that I worked in New York, not exactly the center of friendliness in the world.
- We had Sprints and Spikes and Sprint Loading meetings, where everyone was expected to voice their opinions and fully engage
- On Fridays, we officially stopped working after 4 pm and held a session of "show and tell" where people were encouraged to show off what they had worked on for that week. Internally known as "glimpse," we all wandered around the office, some people barefoot, some juggling things, some doing both, all the while drinking beers and having a lot of fun
- By the way, the beer selection process was completely "open sourced" too, and everyone had a chance to vote for their favorite beers, choosing from several categories: IPA, Light, Non-alcoholic, etc

I immediately became fascinated with the culture of the place and couldn't believe my luck at being able to find a place like it.

Once the honeymoon period quickly passed, I soon realized that I was entirely out of my element! Everyone and I mean everyone in the company was extremely well versed on the use of GNU/Linux, Python and version control tools, while I was still taking my first steps in those areas. Everyone, except for one or two people, was a VIM user, while I was still using GEdit, a graphical text editor. Everyone was also genuinely passionate about the products they were developing, something that I was not used to seeing.

Furthermore, I had been hired to work on a web-based application that used TurboGears and both of those areas were entirely new for me; my background was developing backend code that talked to databases or desktop applications for Windows users. I felt like a sore thumb, sticking out all the time, showing off my "n00bness" and not being able to blend in.

People around me were very accommodating and provided me with plenty of chances and opportunities to learn, and they took it easy on the new guy (I was hire #16 for them). During my first few Sprints, they gave me the easy tasks and honestly cheered me on to celebrate my small successes. In other words, I had all the right ingredients to grow and become a part of the team, and there was no lack of opportunities for someone willing to work hard enough.

Work hard is what I did, day in, day out, but the learning curve was showing to be too steep. I also put a tremendous amount of pressure on myself to perform at the same level as my peers, but that too, slowly became too much for me to handle. Okay, there were some impressive big names from the open source community working there, but I couldn't even perform at the same level as some of the much younger folks.

So I started underperforming and missed my Sprint deliverables a few times. No matter how much support I received from my manager, I could not help and shake off the feeling that I was not helping my team and that I was letting people down. I thought that I was working as hard as I could to catch up with all the learning I needed to do, but what I did was build a wall between my teammates and me.

From this point onward, whenever I faced a hard or new task, instead of trying to solve it, I chose to blame others for my inability to get the job done. If someone offered me help or some guidance, I thought that they were doing it out of pity, which only made me reject their aid and add yet another layer to my wall.

Those were not very happy days for me, but I am sure that my teammates were not having a ton of fun with me around either. To this day I still don't know how they put up with me and kept giving me a chance to redeem myself. Luckily, their willingness to provide me with an opportunity to change my ways was just long enough to allow me to have an epiphany!

The Epiphany

In a yet another example of how your life can be completely turned upside down due to the smallest choices we make, I came across a turning point in my career, and turns out, in my life as well.

I believe that it was in 2008 when my good friend Vinny from Massachusetts flew down to visit for a couple of days. He had another friend who happened to live in the area, and he figured he could see a couple of his old friends in one single trip.

Once he got to North Carolina, we planned to go out and have a cup of coffee to catch up and chat for a while. We ended up meeting at a Barnes and Noble store (to this day one of my favorite places to meet with people), and for the next 90 minutes, I poured my entire heart out to him. I complained about my life decisions, whined about the problems I had at work, and blamed and pointed fingers at everyone from work for being the ones responsible for my failures.

I have to hand it to him. He was a good listener and a good friend, letting me vent all of my frustrations and anger while he calmly sipped his coffee, never once trying to stop me. At the end of our one-sided chat, we went our separate ways: him, probably to a place where he could shake off all of my problems and complains; as for me, I drove home, utterly exhausted from my venting session.

It wasn't until I finally parked the car outside my apartment, and turned off the ignition that reality sank in. It was only then that I saw for the first time what my friend Vinny (and probably everyone else) had seen: the source of my problems were not my teammates or others; the problem was my inability or unwillingness to hold myself accountable to my own mistakes and failures!

Digging Myself out of a Hole

Looking back to the day I had my epiphany, it is interesting to me how quickly I accepted my self-diagnosis and, more impressive, how fast I came up with a solution to my problem.

The very first step I took toward rehabilitating myself was to change my attitude toward my peers. Whereas before I would approach all and every conversation or meeting with a cynical outlook, I decided there and then to become a more optimistic person. I know, it sounds too easy to say these words, but as far as I saw it, I had no alternative but to start assuming positive intent from everyone.

Previously, when meeting with peers, I would come prepared to point fingers at them for whatever I perceived as faults worse than mine. Now, I cleared my mind of all those thoughts, took a deep breath, and literally walked in with the most sincere smile I could muster.

The "trick" was that the smile and attitude of assuming positive intent had to be genuine. If for whatever reason I allowed a little bit of my old habit to take over and control how I talked to someone, I could feel my body tense, my hands turn into fists, and the meeting was pretty much done for me right there.

Once I changed my behavior, and people started feeling more comfortable giving me constructive feedback during our interactions, one of the first positive outcomes I noticed was that my stress was much lower than before. Even when I did receive negative feedback, I still managed not to get too hung up over the negative parts and looked for what the real message was. Instead of thinking "this person always hated me anyway," or "he never appreciated my hard work," I chose to tell myself "I know he means well, and though his words may not be what I want to hear, let me focus on what he is really trying to tell me here."

You'd be surprised how many times I was able to walk from a meeting with a list of "areas for improvement" instead of a list of annoyances and frustrations. Even during my weekly one-on-one sessions with my manager, I made a point of asking for what I could do more or less of to improve myself. Since she could see it in my face and attitude that I meant it, it became noticeably easier for her to give me constructive feedback.

Every week I went over her advice from our previous discussion, asked again what I could change to improve, and walked away with a smile on my face. After a couple of weeks, she told me to continue doing what I was doing already. I had finally reached a point where I became a valuable member of her team!

The next item for me to tackle was my inability to learn about our technology as well as become more proficient on GNU/Linux, Python, and Agile methodologies. So I embraced my ignorance and for the first time since I joined the company, I made a conscious decision to start from the bottom.

I started arriving at work before 8 am (I used to "clock in" at 9 am before) and leaving well past 6 pm. During those extra hours I was putting in, I started following and reading every single commit emails from the multiple products we were developing. For a while, it felt like drinking from the fire hose, but after a couple of weeks something clicked, and I started to see patterns emerge.

During our daily scrums, I became acutely aware of what my peers were talking about, how all the different pieces fit tightly together into a more meaningful solution, and who had the expertise on what areas. Eventually, if someone was blocking someone else or something had gotten broken overnight, I was able to comment on what commit was the culprit.

Following closely what other developers from other groups were working on became a strong skill for me and something that helped me become more in tune with what was happening around me, especially when faced with new challenges or new teams.

One more final change to how I went about my working hours was my decision to take on whatever task was available that nobody else wanted to do.

No matter how simple, mundane, complicated or scary, whenever someone needed something to be done, and nobody else wanted to do it, I'd raise my hand and volunteer for the job. Not only was I ready to accept my ignorance but I was also eager for whatever new learning opportunities came my way!

Thanks to this new mentality, I once became the "release nanny," or the person whose task is to remind everyone of all the different assignments, and their order, required to prepare the product for release. All I had to go by were some notes from the previous "nanny" and the encouragement from some of my teammates who were probably surprised to see me willingly getting out of my comfort zone.

Another example of something entirely new I volunteered to work on was testing some of the more advanced end-to-end customer scenarios, which required a deeper understanding of our technologies. The way I saw it, since I wanted to learn about this topic anyway, what better way to do it than when people were counting on you! Sure, it sounds scary to think about doing something utterly alien, knowing that people are counting on you, but all I saw were opportunities opening for me.

Through the next few weeks and months that went by, I became more and more comfortable with my role of apprentice, and since I was no longer putting pressure on myself, I believe that I reached that point where nothing scared me anymore. My mind was wide open to handle that massive learning curve which only a couple of months before had me whining about life.

The Layoffs

Around 2008, with the economic downturn caused by the housing bubble, the company was forced to make its first massive layoff, and with that first round, I saw some of our most talented engineers pack up their things and walk out the door. I confess that I was shocked that my name did not come up and I kept expecting that some huge mistake had taken place and someone had forgotten to tell me that I had been fired too.

We all coped with the situation as best as someone working on a startup can, which usually means that you start working on more things to pick up the "slack" left by those who went. Our working hours began to stretch into the early evening hours, but since I was already working until 6 pm, I didn't feel any difference and continued working just as hard as before.

Not long after we had all gotten back to a normal rhythm, we were surprised with yet another round of layoffs, and this time I wasn't even present to witness it. I had taken a day off that day to nurse a nasty cold when my phone rang. It was the vice president of engineering who wanted to tell me about the company's decision to let go more people due to their new strategy and product roadmap.

I was prepared to hear him tell me not to go back to work, but he surprised me when he said that I should not be worried about my role and that they were pleased to continue having me working as their Quality Engineer. It was with a sigh of relief that I hung up the phone and embraced my wife, knowing that I had just dodged a bullet.

For the next two years, the remaining engineering team, about 11 of us if I'm not mistaken, set out with enthusiasm to build the technology that would identify our company as the visionaries and trendsetters that we were. Due to the size of the team, we now had to work as fast, as agile and as effective as never before. That also meant that we worked until late in the evenings, often working weekends as well to make sure that we met our deadlines.

I have never worked so hard or so long as I did during the next two years, and yet, despite being tired, or sometimes frustrated with some technical setbacks, we all showed up for work and gave our 110%. I don't recall anyone ever complaining or whining about working until 2 am and having to be back in the office by 8 am that same day. We were a well-oiled machine and milestone, after milestone, we kept delivering the updates and features requested by our customers.

If before I was looking for opportunities to learn and explore uncharted territories, it was during this period that I learned the most and was able to take advantage of all the opportunities that came up:

First, I became a core developer for one of the GNU/Linux distributions we maintained ourselves called Foresight. Since Foresight GNU/Linux was built on the technologies we developed, and since that was the distribution that I used every day to do my work, it was vital that I could rely on it every single day. It was also crucial for me to learn as much about our technology as possible so that I could resolve my problems and not find myself blocked.

Learning enough about our technologies also gave me an opportunity to play with the idea of maintaining my own GNU/Linux distribution (I never shared it with anyone though) and building several GNU/Linux Appliances along the way.

If you're not familiar with the term "appliance," it may be easier to think about how one can play different games in their gaming console. Just as one can put a new game CD or DVD into their console, one can also get an application to run on top of an operating system or deployed on a cloud environment, without having to know how to install or configure it.

So I built and maintained appliances for Django and **Transifex**, a well-known translations web-based application that required many compilation and configuration steps as well as the knowledge of how to get all the required dependencies (e.g., web server and databases) to work together. If anyone, including the Transifex developers, wanted to try out their new version quickly, they could easily provision an instance on Amazon's EC2 and start playing with it in less than one minute!

My involvement with the **GNOME** project also took off as we helped package and test their development branches, and eventually, I ran and won a seat for their **Board of Directors**, a position I maintained for the entire duration of the expected tenure. Though I can't say that I enjoyed the experience (we went through some turbulent times, including some friction with Canonical, the company behind Ubuntu Linux), I did meet a lot of passionate open source enthusiasts and got to see things from a completely different perspective.

The combination of all of these factors added to my newly found passion for test automation with Python. Coupled with the many tools we built to drive our releases, it gave me the final and most important ingredient that I needed to elevate myself from working on Quality Assurance to becoming a defacto Quality Engineer: DevOps methodologies.

I now felt that I was ready to take on any challenge that came my way, and it was just the right time too, for one of the most significant opportunities of my professional career was about to knock at my door.

Apprenticeship Patterns

Many were the times I wished there was a manual that explained to me how to turn my career around. Did I have to learn things by going through a "school of hard knocks?" I often felt that there had to be a better, smarter way.

It turns out that there is at least one book I'm aware of that may fit in the category of helping someone to get a hold of their career and self-improvement: "Apprenticeship Patterns: Guidance for the Aspiring Software Craftsman," by David H. Hoover and Adewale Oshineye.

Chockfull of useful advice to help you hone soft skills and learning techniques, this book provides valuable behavior patterns than one can emulate and learn from to perfect one's "craft." Some of the topics discussed include:

- Expose Your Ignorance
- Confront Your Ignorance
- Be the Worst
- Sweep the Floor
- Find Mentors
- and many more!

Does this list look a lot like some of the behavior changes I introduced to my life when I felt that it had reached the very bottom?

By the time I read it, thanks to a tip from a co-worker who was familiar with the "Sweep the Floor" pattern, it was already December of 2017, and I had just recently been promoted to Senior Manager of Quality Engineering at my current job. I remember feeling astounded at how someone had been able to capture all of my early career struggles so thoroughly and how I had unknowingly used the same patterns from the book to deal with them!

Though I take great pride in the way that I managed to overcome the many obstacles I encountered during my transition to becoming a Quality Engineer, if you recognized some of my struggles and are still looking for a way to overcome them, I can't recommend "Apprenticeship Patterns" highly enough!

If you're starting on your journey in the world of software engineering, be that as a developer or a tester, I believe the patterns covered in this book will be instrumental to your career and sanity. Even if you consider yourself a more "seasoned" engineer, you may still find some great little gems buried in there.

In the next part of this book, I will explore some of the soft and technical skills which have served me well these last ten years and which I hope will be just as useful to you as well.

Swim or Sink

When I first joined Red Hat to work as a Quality Engineer for a brand new product, I faced an interesting situation: the product was written in Rails, had a command line tool written in Python, and the existing QE team was using Clojure and Java for their current automated tests. Having spent the last few years working mostly with Python, this diverse environment made the onboarding process a little bit more challenging for me.

Shortly after my first week of orientation, the person who I was supposed to shadow and teach me the ropes went on a one week vacation, followed by a month-long stint working remotely from Brazil.

Also, since the office was pretty close to being at full capacity, I had no official desk to sit at and had to "camp out" at someone else's for the first two days while my manager, who worked remotely from California, tried to find me a more permanent space. When I was finally assigned a spot, it was not together with my new team but with a completely different group, in a completely different part of the building. I guess you could say that it didn't feel very welcoming and I started questioning my decision to leave my previous job.

I spent the first few weeks getting to know as many people from our group as I could and trying to learn about our product, processes, and goals. I have to confess that doing all of these things without having someone to guide me was a bit daunting. I had no idea who my teammates were or where they sat, which in hindsight was probably a good thing since it forced me to explore the building and start introducing myself to whoever I came across.

Eventually, this would pay off big time as it helped me build a stable relationship with people from many different groups, some of them becoming good friends even though we worked on different products.

Once I became more familiar with my entire team, I proceeded to spend a few intensive weeks learning about the product and how to leverage the existing automation framework to write more automated test cases. Remember how I mentioned that both Clojure and Java were used? The way things were designed, you had to pick either Clojure for web UI automation or Java for command line automation.

I have to be honest with you, Java was never one of my favorite programming languages. Also, I knew absolutely nothing about Clojure, so I found myself facing a couple of tough decisions:

- overcome my bias against coding in Java and

- learning how to switch from imperative to functional programming in an entirely new language.

Given a choice, I would have chosen to go with RSpec or some other Ruby-friendly language, but I was the new guy and in no position to negotiate... yet.

Sadly, neither my mentor (the person who went on vacation the week after I started) nor my fellow QE teammates, some local and some working from India, were very helpful or welcoming, and I grew very frustrated with my inability to make progress. There were many unknowns for me and the most basic thing, such as learning where to get the source code for our testing framework could take a couple of days for me to achieve.

People either didn't know the answer (which was scary since these were the people who were supposed to be writing automated tests) or never bothered to learn since they were against the idea of using Clojure or Java! Think about it for a minute: some of the paid employees made the conscious decision to boycott the testing framework because they did not agree with the choice of using a specific technology over something they preferred! What were they doing instead then, you may be asking yourself? I honestly don't know... It was mind-blowing!

I visited the local Barnes and Noble bookstore, purchased a copy of a Clojure programming book (I think the first one ever published, back in early 2012) and spent the next couple of weeks learning about its syntax and undergoing a major, self-inflicted paradigm shift as my mind started to get used to functional programming. If you're an old hand LISP programmer, this may not be a big deal for you, but for someone whose major programming languages had been Visual Basic, PL/SQL, and Python, this was a pretty significant change for me.

Since I was still on my "probation" period, I decided to learn as much as I could and as fast as possible so that I could start showing some progress. After spending the first three months where my daily stand up call status was "Still learning about X or Y," I couldn't wait to start being productive and add value to our team.

Now, I like to think of myself as someone who is capable of learning new programming languages and new technologies pretty quickly, but even after knowing enough about Clojure to the point where I could read and understand code, learning how to use the framework itself was yet another learning curve for me.

By then my mentor had returned from his vacation and we spent many hours together where he tried to sell me on the beauty of the framework, how clever Clojure code can be and how using Emacs would improve my Clojure code writing experience (which I have to agree to, since writing LISP-like code on Vim was painful).

I have to give him credit for being very patient and doing his best to help me get up to speed. I feel that he did his best and there was never a time where I didn't think that he was genuinely trying to help me. He also turned me from a loyal user of Vim to a new disciple of Emacs!

But the one thing I could never shake off was the fact that adding new functionality to the framework required some deep understanding of the entire source code, and such changes were never trivial to make. There was also the fact that very few people in our team were using it for the same reasons, so we had a pretty lean adoption rate from our own quality engineers!

Lastly, there was also the problem of hiring new talent if we were ever to expand the team. Back in early 2012, there weren't many quality engineers out there with a solid understanding of Clojure for web UI automation.

If my teammates were avoiding doing web UI automation, the story for command line tool testing wasn't too different either, though most of them didn't feel the same aversion about Java as they had for Clojure.

The way test cases were written and even how they were executed was not very straightforward and required some specific knowledge about the environment (e.g., the servers being used, how to configure some variables). For the few who had built that framework from the beginning, it was trivial to add new test cases, but for anyone starting new like I was, many unknowns were not documented anywhere and lived in someone else's mind.

Feeling my frustration getting the best of me, and never being one who is afraid to speak up about my opinions, I told my manager about the many pitfalls that I saw waiting for us in the not so distant future if we kept doing things the way we had been thus far. What we needed, I told him, was to scrap everything and start anew!

Let Them Who Never Created Their Own Framework Cast the First Stone

Having told my manager my pessimistic views about our existing testing framework and how nobody, other than the people who created it was using it during their day to day activities, I found myself confronted by my mentor. You know, the guy who loved Clojure. My manager had shared with him my opinions and, unsurprisingly, he wasn't very pleased.

I tried to have a non-biased, logical conversation with him, and explain what I thought the pitfalls were of using a mixture of Clojure and Java for automated tests, but he was not having any of it. We covered many different aspects of what a testing framework should and should not have to improve its adoption and usability, but he was firmly convinced that what we had was the best option, and since he was one level above me, end of story.

But I was not ready to give up yet and continued to try to make my point over many lengthy discussions. Eventually, he threw down the gauntlet and proclaimed: No matter what technology we bring to this group, I challenge anyone to create something as useful and as feature-complete as what we have right now in Clojure. That's when the stubborn part of me said, 'hold my beer.'

What so far had been an informal challenge became an actual request from our manager, who quickly realized that he had a tricky situation in his hands: should he continue letting the team doing things the same way that they had been, or should he listen to the new guy, i.e., me, and get the entire team onto a new platform? For some reason, and to this day I don't quite know why, he chose the latter.

The very next day after my last discussion with my mentor, I was called into a meeting with the team over the phone (back then we still didn't use video conferencing), and our manager proposed a contest: could anyone in the group write a complete testing framework in one week? The rules were as follows:

- The framework had to provide the same set of features as the existing one written in Clojure
- Automated tests had to support a data-driven approach. In other words, instead of having to write multiple tests where only the input data changed, you

would write one test and allow for it to take ion a varied number of different data types

- The framework had to be fully documented

All proposals would be reviewed by a small committee of other managers, and the winning selection would be chosen to replace the existing framework. If no proposal could match all the requirements, then nothing would change, and everyone would then be forced to continue using the current tools.

Sounds pretty scary, wouldn't you agree? But having spent the last four years taking on all kinds of crazy and complicated tasks at my previous job, I didn't think twice. I quickly volunteered to spend the next week to tackle the challenge using Python and the Robot framework, followed by two more people who also volunteered to do the same using Python and Groovy.

The next seven days (weekend included) were a blur, a hectic schedule of cranking out lots and lots of code, adding documentation and getting things built on Github. I even took the time to implement a pipeline where the documentation was automatically generated on every commit (something that we may take for granted these days but it was a bit of a novelty for some folks in 2012.)

By late Sunday afternoon I was pretty exhausted, and even though I had not been able to implement every single required feature into my new framework, I felt that what I had was very solid and had a chance of getting people's attention. The rest of the functionality could easily be added later on if more time was available so that I could type the code for it.

Monday morning we all gathered together to show off the proposals to our manager. Unfortunately, the person who wanted to use Groovy gave up, but there was another proposal written in Python to compete with mine.

I don't remember who went first, but before we got to the end of the meeting, it was pretty evident to everyone that the two proposals had accomplished in seven days almost everything that the existing framework had achieved in months of development.

Even though none of the proposals had feature parity with the Clojure framework, it was only a matter of a little time and resources to get it done. In the end, I was able to "sell" my framework as the one that should replace both Clojure and Java tools we had, and I was selected the winner of the contest.

Despite feeling vindicated and, who am I kidding, pretty proud of myself for being able to accomplish this feat in seven days and under pressure, I was the new guy in the group, and I couldn't afford to come across as being smug and a show-off. I had to work with these people, and the last thing I wanted was to make enemies at my new job. Luckily for me, my manager agreed that instead of dropping the current framework right away, we should try a more gradual approach and look for the right moment to start transitioning people to work on the new tool.

Since the upstream name for the product we worked on was Katelo and the new framework leveraged the Robot Test framework, I called the new project Robotello (I don't remember why I chose to add the extra 'L,' but I never changed it afterward).

I then made it public on Github and switched my focus once again back to our product and the release looming large ahead of us. The opportunity to turn my focus 100% on developing Robotello would come up earlier than I expected.

The Rebirth of Robotello

The thing about working on a new, not thoroughly planned and designed product that relies on an upstream project not under your control is that you never know what tomorrow will bring you. For someone writing automated functional tests for such an upstream project, that means that every day could be the day where all your hard work can become obsolete or worthless with a single decision.

The "doomsday" for our team arrived the day when our program team decided to leverage the existing TheForeman project to become the primary delivery platform for our product. To be clear: the project itself was pretty solid and mature; the problem was due to something else completely which you will see shortly.

Mind you that back then I was not in a position to argue for or against the decision, so I will have to believe that all pros and cons were weighed and all alternatives were considered before the decision was made. But that day marked the day when all of our existing web UI and command line interface automated tests became worthless!

How does an automated test become worthless, you may ask? In my definition, an automated test, or any task for that matter, becomes worthless when the effort to update it or maintain it becomes too "expensive" for your team to maintain. By switching the main web interface for our product from Katelo to TheForeman, all the web locators that our UI tests depended on became obsolete. All of them!

If you're not familiar with how web UI automation works, you can think of it this way: imagine that you have a text field and a button you need to interact with to simulate a real customer using a web application. We'll call the text field, button and any other visual object found on a web page a web element.

The first thing one must do is to be able to identify the location of a web element programmatically, and there are many ways of doing this. The easiest way would be to rely on a unique CSS ID because they are supposed to be, well, unique. So if you know that a button has a CSS ID of "submit," then you can use your automation framework to find this element on a web page identified by the ID of "submit." From this point onward, you can interact with this element, and since we're referring to a button, one could click it programmatically, or check whether it is enabled, for example.

The problem arises when a web application is not designed and implemented for automated testing, which usually means that web elements are not assigned unique

CSS IDs. This problem is relatively common in my experience, and one is then forced to get creative about how to identify the location of a web element. Most of the time this means that you'll have to devise an XPath expression that pinpoints their location based on their relative or absolute position inside the web page's Document Object Model (DOM).

These types of expressions can be just as powerful as using CSS IDs, but if the web page ever goes under any update where the position of an element changes, then your XPath expression needs to be updated or your automation won't be able to find it anymore.

Even though we could probably have spent the time to update every single web locator in our automation, with the decision to switch to TheForeman, the menus and page workflows for our product were so completely affected that there was no way of shortcutting the effort to salvage our tests.

Furthermore, the existing command line tool, written initially in Python, would be switched to Ruby. Since our automated tests for it relied on being able to import certain Python modules to interact with the product, our entire test suite was no longer useful.

After a quick chat with my manager a verdict was declared: let's take advantage of the unfortunate situation, resurrect Robotello, my Python testing framework from the dead, and rewrite all of our approximately 800 automated tests!

This was around Thanksgiving of 2013 and since I had some days of vacation coming up coupled with the fact that we close our office the last week of December, I asked for my manager's permission to spend the next few weeks rethinking and designing how we could get web UI AND command line automated tests to use the same tool.

If you remember from previous chapters, web UI tests were written in Clojure and command line interface ones were written in Java. Additionally, I wanted to add support for testing the REST API too.

My primary objectives for Robotello were:

- It had to be easy to install and deploy: I wanted anyone to be able to clone the source code and use it to automate test cases without having to depend on any third-party dependencies, systems or specific environments.
- It had to be easy to use: I wanted for the framework itself to be dead easy to use, following an object-oriented pattern that would allow one to use methods

with intuitive nomenclature and smart default values. If one wanted for example to create a new user, the code should look like new_user = User.create()

- It had to be flexible: The framework should allow one to write web UI, command line or REST API automated tests without requiring different libraries or syntax. In other words, the syntax new_user = User.create() should allow me to create a new user via any of the interfaces.

That month of December 2013 was the busiest period of my career regarding writing new code and building something from scratch. After some consideration, I decided to drop the Robot library from the code, added Paramiko and Selenium as new dependencies and set out to create a whole new set of modules to support my needs.

I think that this was also the most fun period as a quality engineer that I ever had in my career! By the time we came back from the holidays in early January, I had the initial implementation and support for all three interfaces ready and committed to our code repository.

Hindsight Is 20/20

Now that I had Robotello ready for some serious usage, the next task for me was to start a series of hands-on meetings where I could demo to my teammates how to rewrite our current tests using Robotello. Despite my initial fear of a strong pushback by some of our engineers, I was pleasantly surprised at the warm reception it received.

Right out of the gate the feedback I received was that the object-oriented, Pythonic syntax was by far more straightforward to use and understand, and within the first couple of days of showing it off, I received a couple of change requests from my teammates who submitted improvements to the runtime configuration module and even some tests!

The relatively quick success Robotello achieved within our team helped me convince everyone that Python was a good solution for our needs, including our in-house Clojure and Java gurus. Even though I was the only person in our team who knew how to code in Python, it didn't take long for my teammates to learn it, which reinforced my belief that in the long run, it would be easier to hire and onboard quality engineers from all walks of life. Finding solid candidates who knew Clojure and had a background in quality engineering was nearly impossible to accomplish.

Most importantly, the speed with which my fellow teammates started adopting and contributing to the project and the overall quick progress that we made converting the existing 800 automated tests did not go unnoticed by my manager. Sometime around the middle of 2013, my hard work was recognized and awarded with a career-changing promotion to Associate Manager!

As I adapted to my new role and responsibilities, and while still heavily influenced by the quick results we were getting with Robotello, I made a decision that at the time I felt was vital to our ability to provide high testing coverage of our product: ensure that all interfaces were exercised by our tests.

So for every automated functional test we wrote, the same test had to be executed through all three interfaces: web, command line and REST interfaces. One could import the desired module for an interface, write a single test, and have it execute against our product with only a couple of lines of code. To run the same test against a different interface, one had just to use the same test, make sure to import the appropriate interface module and voila!

In about six months of intense development, we were able to rewrite the original 800 automated tests. Additionally, we were able to make them all data-driven, which means that whereas before only one single type of data was being used for every one of them, we now had a series of different inputs to pass to our tests. We caught many issues related to non-ASCII characters by switching to this data-driven process, and we were all feeling pretty good about ourselves.

As the months passed by and more features were added to our product, the number of automated tests added to our automation also grew and pretty soon we were executing a few thousand tests every time a new build was delivered by our developers. Our Jenkins was continually getting called into action, and for a while, we were all busy and focused on adding more testing coverage to our ever evolving, ever changing product.

I was so caught up with the fever of seeing the number of automated tests going up every week, that despite my best intentions I completely missed a couple of warning signs from our Jenkins dashboards. How could more tests be a bad thing, right?

Well, first of all, we were running our entire test suite against all versions of our product without any type of prioritization or plan. We all thought, or at least I did, that

90

throwing all we had against a build was the right thing to do, as it would allow us to quickly identify any regressions introduced since the last build. Emphasis on the word "quickly."

The problem was that running a few thousand automated tests takes time, especially if you're running them sequentially. While early on the entire test suite could take a couple of hours to complete, we were now talking about eight or more. If a significant regression was found by the automation, it could take at least until the next day for someone to notice it. One of the main advantages for letting computers run test automation is to get results as quickly as possible, and we were definitely not doing that anymore.

Also, since more tests were being run, the process of reviewing failures now took much longer to complete, a tedious and sometimes manual and error-prone process. When the product is not undergoing a lot of changes, you may get a couple dozen failures every now and then, but if massive changes are taking place, you may find yourself staring at a few hundred failures to review.

If you can't quickly access them and identify whether the underlying problems are real defects (aka. "bugs") or issues with your tests, your team could get into deep trouble rather quickly. This problem can be further exacerbated during the release phase, when the time between finding issues, fixing and retesting them may require rapid turnaround from everyone!

We found ourselves working for the automation instead of having the automation working for us, and something had to be done before it was too late!

NOT All Of Your Tests Are Belong To Us

The plan to improve our automation and help speed up the time it took us to deliver reliable test results required some planning, but there were a couple of quick, easy wins which we had been too busy to notice.

First of all, there was no real need for us to run our tests sequentially! If I remember correctly, the only reason why we started doing that was that there weren't that many tests early on. Seriously, we were so eager to see our tests running that we never even considered not running them one after the other. I know, embarrassing.

Luckily the Robotello framework had been designed to allow for tests to be run in parallel, and with a quick tweak to our configuration file, this problem was quickly remedied. From beginning to end, running the entire test suite was now back to reasonable hours, but the number of failures had almost that quadrupled! There was something fishy going on.

The entire team spent a couple of days investigating all the failures, pouring through the many megabytes of logs spewed by the automation, looking for a culprit. By the time we finally arrived at it, we experienced both a feeling of relief, for finding the problem, and one of frustration for having neglected to consider a crucial factor in our testing strategy.

It turns out that there were some APIs called by the web UI and the command line tool that were not asynchronous, which meant that every time they were called, the entire application would have to pause and wait for something to be returned. While we were running our tests sequentially, we never experienced this problem since a new test could only execute once the previous one had finished running. But now that we had a total of sixteen processes running our tests in parallel, many of them would merely timeout, blocked on some pending test that was stuck still waiting for something else to finish. Facepalm!

We now had a different problem that needed to be fixed quickly. Having automated tests is fantastic but only as long as you can rely on them. Once again we all rallied to investigate the problem and after some discussions came up with a couple of possible solutions:

- Request that our development team fix the code to make those APIs async, or
- Further split how to execute our tests, separating those that could run parallelized from the ones that

failed with a timeout, and run them sequentially once all other tests had finished

Now it was the development team's turn to do their research and figure out how much time it would take them to make those APIs asynchronous. By the time they came back to us with their answer, we had learned that to make the changes, a great deal of the core functionality around those APIs would have to be rewritten, something that was way too risky to do at that time. With no other alternative, we started refactoring our execution plan to split our tests once again.

With this problem resolved, we turned our attention back to the execution time, looking for ways to cut a few more minutes out of the whole process. Since a lot of times when we saw massive failures, they were usually caused by regressions in the product's core functionality itself, it didn't make sense for us to run the entire suite if we already knew that there were some critical problems.

What we needed was to leverage what we already had and create an "early warning system" to alert us of these types of problems right away. If, for example, you knew that the login functionality through the web UI was broken, then why run all other tests when you can't even log in? It made much more sense to test that core functionality first, and only proceed with all other UI tests if this basic test passed. Otherwise, fail right away and don't bother to run the rest.

The team identified which of our existing tests could be used to create a "smoke" test suite, and once we had a robust subset, we made a point of running them right away, as soon as a new build arrived through our automated pipeline. Now, when a significant regression was introduced between builds, we were able to see it and alert our counterparts in the development team in less than thirty minutes. This change alone played a significant role in increasing our trust that the builds being delivered were of a higher quality, but it also helped improve the relationship between quality engineers and developers.

Next on our list of improvements was to rethink our data-driven approach. Sure, throwing all types of input data into our automated tests allowed us to cover a much wider area of functionality, making sure that the application did a decent job at sanitizing the data that users were feeding into it. But this also meant that a test now took n-times longer to execute, where n represents how many different data types of input we used. A decision we came up with was to only focus on using the UTF8 characters set, the logic being that it would be the best representation for the type of input our users would enter.

There were some other areas of optimization that we tackled during our effort to improve the runtime of our automated test suite. While I could go through all of them individually here, I prefer to focus on something that we're still working on right now which I feel is a common pitfall for many new teams working on quality engineering.

Remember how I had decided early on to run the same tests against the three different interfaces of our application? Well, as I mentioned before, as the number of automated tests goes up, so does the time it takes for all of them to complete. When we're talking about running a few thousand of these bad boys, every single second you can save is a blessing to be counted.

In practice, REST API tests are by far the fastest type of test that you can execute. There is no overhead required, and as long as you have a clean, standard and reliable API to run your tests against, I highly recommend that you build your test suite with this type of test as much as possible. For the most part, these should run very quickly, and if your suite is taking more than a couple of hours, you may want to revise them. I feel that for our product, this is very much a done deal for us and we rely pretty heavily on our API tests.

Next, assuming that you have to test a command line tool, which we did, I recommend that you focus your automation here. If this command line tool was designed to leverage the existing REST API, then you're in luck since your current REST API tests should already give you an excellent base and enough confidence that the core functionality is working as expected. In this case, then, your job is to complement your API tests and instead of checking the most basic functionality, focus on building more integration and system tests instead.

In our case, we still have a large number of automated tests that execute the command line tool, checking that the most basic commands work, followed by a significant but not as large body of integration and system tests. It is certainly a laudable goal to aim for a high level of testing coverage but when we're talking about a few thousand of automated tests, keeping them up to date when the command line tool consistently changes from release to release is very painful. Given a choice, I'd instead focus on being more selective about what type of tests I implement for this type of interface and would go for a more complementary approach than try to have parity with the API tests.

Lastly, we come to the web UI automation tests, the most fragile and irksome type of test that a quality engineer has to deal with when working with a web application! Web UI automation requires a great deal of patience, creativity, and sanity since chances are that whenever you see a lot of failures in your automation, the bulk of them will be related to a change in the web UI!

If you imagine that the distribution of your tests should resemble a pyramid, the bulk of your API tests will make up its base, followed by a substantial number of command line tool tests in the middle. Then the very tip of it should be made up of the types of tests that are either too expensive to maintain or take too long to execute, like UI tests.

For the last five months, we had added over one thousand web UI automated tests to our test suite, covering pretty much every single page and workflow for our product. However, whenever new changes were introduced into the web UI, such as moving a horizontal menu of items to a vertical one, most if not all of our tests would fail. Once we got past the login page, our web locators for the menus wouldn't match the new values. Just like that, our tests would timeout and eventually fail.

Taking advantage of an opportunity that came up when a recent UI change broke our UI tests again, I decided to bite the bullet and redesign them. The idea was simple: starting with the most basic, core functionality of our application, identify the web pages involved in these workflows and automate that first! In other words, instead of fixing our tests that would attempt to Create, Read (aka. search), Update or Delete a user, for example, focus on a complete scenario that would exercise all of these different functionalities and allow us to maintain it all as a single test. Do that across the board, starting with the most critical areas, and the total number of UI tests should decrease significantly.

Now, I know that having these types of tests as independent entities could simplify identifying if a problem only affects the update process and not necessarily the creation or deletion. There indeed is a price to pay for perhaps oversimplifying your testing strategy, but I feel that with proper logging and a more robust design for your tests, you can get the same value with one single test than multiple ones.

You may find my decision a bit controversial, and if you do, I'd love to hear your thoughts about it. I believe that if your web application makes extensive use of the underlying REST API, then your existing "smoke" and component tests (the ones forming the base and middle of your pyramid) should catch any regressions or defects introduced by new development. Keeping your UI tests down to a manageable minimum has the added advantage of letting you spend less time dealing with false failures and focusing your efforts where it may matter the most.

Our team is still making changes to how we test our products, and I feel that we've just scratched the surface. It may sound a bit daunting to you hear me saying this, but to be honest, getting a product to be thoroughly tested automatically is like the Holy Grail of quality engineering. We all want to get it, but it is a long and arduous journey to get there, and you may never get it in the end.

Just as critical as having stable, robust and reliable automated tests is the need to have them executed at the right time and while the product is still being designed and developed, and that is what I'll talk about next.

Everybody To The Left

Improving our testing framework and decreasing the runtime for the execution of our tests proved to be an excellent move for our team. Ss we increased the frequency with which we released new versions of our product and pushed updates to our customers, we started feeling pretty good about the outcome of our hard work.

The first positive sign we saw coming out of our refactoring was that the release team responsible for building and delivering testable builds for our products incorporated our "smoke" test suite into their processes. While we had relied on these tests to catch critical regressions in the builds delivered to the QE team, this step only happened **after** the release team had completed their tasks. So, for every "dead on arrival" build we identified, it could take at least a couple of extra days for the development team to fix the issue and for the whole thing to get rebuilt.

Regressions between builds are sadly not that uncommon, and depending on how severe they are and how long it takes to fix them, you could be losing precious time waiting for things to get ready for you.

Within just a couple of weeks of adding our "smoke" tests to the release pipeline, the number of broken builds we received started to decrease significantly. The QE team did not have to spring into action until everything looked good and the automation for the release process itself was "green." I can't stress enough how important and critical it is to have a reliable build process for a product. If you can't tell with any level of certainty when you can expect the next build for your product or if it will even be fully functional, this is something that needs to get addressed quickly, or you're bound to see some disgruntled people on your team.

While our automation was providing value detecting regressions with our product, by the time we caught them, it was too late in the process. When we moved our tests closer to the "source" of our product, we shortened the feedback loop between building it and testing it, which allowed for a much quicker turnaround for getting better builds. That got me thinking: "If such a simple move could make such a significant improvement to our processes, imagine how much more value we could add if we were to move more of our testing 'upstream?'"

You may be wondering, why wouldn't quality engineers be working closely with the development team to begin with? Haven't I claimed that one of the advantages of being a quality engineer is the fact that you want to provide guidance and be involved as early as possible in the Software Lifecycle Development Process? Well, for better or worse, some companies consider automated tests their "secret sauce," and no matter if their product is open sourced or not, they do not want to part with their tests.

There may be other reasons as to why a team of quality engineers is not working "upstream" yet, but in our case, it was a matter of changing some minds and adjusting expectations.

While the idea of adding more tests to an upstream project may seem beneficial to anyone, your quality engineers may feel that they would be giving up their control over them. Once you submit your code and it gets merged into an open source project, that code is no longer yours but part of the entire open source community.

I know this should be obvious and logical to most people used to working on an open source project. What may not be as obvious is how a quality engineer may feel about not having full control over what gets tested, what tests are being added or how new tests are getting implemented. Also, when automated tests are maintained upstream, and someone introduces a change that breaks them, who owns the task of fixing it? Is it your team's or the person whose commit broke them?

When you're a quality engineer working for a company that relies on an upstream project, you may feel obligated to fix all broken tests or run the risk of seeing your product and processes downstream suffer later on. Don't despair, however, for even if this is your situation right now, there are ways you can improve things, which I'll talk about a bit later.

Whenever you move your testing and processes closer to the earlier phases of the Software Lifecycle Development Process, you're performing what is called "shift-left testing." While I don't intend to discuss all the pros and cons of using this approach to software testing, I would like to at least talk about why I feel that it is a right decision for many QE teams and why I have decided to implement it across all the QE teams currently under my supervision.

To illustrate the advantages that I see with this approach, assume that you're a quality engineer whose primary responsibility is to work side by side with one or more developers on a brand new feature for your product or project. What could you do at work to ensure that you can have a positive impact as early as possible?

Well, since we're talking about a brand new functionality, the chances are that you won't see a whole lot of development happening during the first couple of weeks. Does that mean that you get a pass and should find something else to work on while the development team figures things out? Absolutely not!

Start by scheduling recurring conversations with your counterparts and reading the requirements for the new feature. If your program team does not have a formal requirements document for you, start asking questions about what the expected functionality should be. What are all the user stories and use cases for it? Is the goal to implement them all within a couple of sprints and deliver it "fully baked" or to provide them in smaller implements through a series of deliverables? Will testing require some specific infrastructure and hardware, or can you leverage what you already know and have?

As you can see, there could be many questions that may need serious thinking and design as early as the very first day that a new feature is handed off to the development team. Asking these types of questions early will not only help you plan your activities ahead of time but also give the entire team a lot to think about before a feature can be considered wholly designed.

After a couple of weeks, assuming you have gotten some answers to your questions, you should be in a position to write down all of your test cases and have a robust test plan for how you will test your feature. These test cases should be continuously reviewed with your development team until your expectations of how they will implement the feature are met. These types of conversations will also give you an opportunity to explain how you will be testing it and make any "special" requests that may be of help to your automation later on, such as adding unique CSS IDs to web elements, for example.

By the fourth or fifth week of development, you should now not only be following the progress for your feature but also be in a position to see all the code changes and even be able to help the development team test them before any code gets committed into the main source code branch. Depending on how far the feature may be at this point, you could even go through your test cases manually and assert that it is working as expected and that it matches all the criteria already established.

It is also around this time that you could start writing the automated tests for your features based on the test cases and manual validation. Sure, you may not have all the functionality fleshed out yet, but you could at least start to create the necessary "scaffolding" for what will become the final automated tests. You don't necessarily need to go crazy and create a ton of automated test cases. Remember that more automation doesn't always equate to higher product quality, but higher quality tests will.

When you get close to the end of the development phase for your product, you and your entire team should feel very confident about the level of completeness, or doneness of your feature, and you should have the tests to prove it. If your tests show that not all test cases are passing, you are also in a position to prove it to your team, at which point it should be pretty evident that things are not ready for prime time yet.

As I hope you can see, shifting to the left is an advantageous methodology because it gives you the best opportunity to make an impact on the design, implementation, and testing of what will become either a new feature or a fix for a customer-facing issue. Instead of waiting on the other side of the proverbial wall separating development from testing, you can pretty much obliterate the wall altogether!

I understand that the scenario I just covered assumes that you have just started working on a project and don't already have other commitments and tasks to go through. Your reality may be entirely different, and you may have additional meetings and deadlines breathing down your neck. If that is the case, I still believe that a schedule or routine close to what I described above is possible. What you need is to have a good time management plan in place!

Before we talk about time management strategies, however, I'd like to talk about some common ideas you can put in place to ensure that you can make a difference in your team and improve the chances of growing your career. When every day can be a challenge, you can either sit back and complain about it, or you can choose to do something!

Be Part of the Solution

A few years back, while browsing the backlog of defects for one of the products I manage, I came across an issue that had been closed by a Quality Engineer the night before with the following comment:

"It doesn't work."

Just like that, the issue was marked as having failed the verification process and automatically re-assigned to the developer responsible for it. In many places, this would probably be the end of the story, but not under my watch!

Your job as a Quality Engineer does not end when you reject the proposed solution to a defect! I understand that the general expectation is not that you will fix the issue yourself (more about this later), but there is so much more than can be done in a situation like this that may surprise you.

Allow me then to expand a little bit more on this by providing a more concrete example. Let's say that we need to verify that the Development group corrected the following defect:

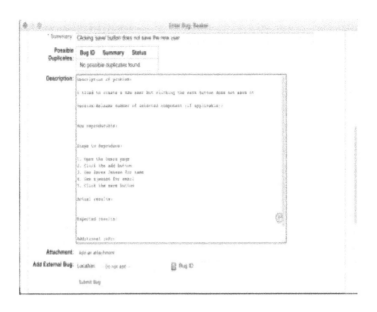

For starters, I have to say that this "bug" report lacks information on many fronts. I mean, I understand that the user Søren Jensen was not saved, but in my opinion, this doesn't give the complete picture. Many times, it is the simplest things that we take for granted that are vital to understanding what could be happening when something does not work as expected. For example:

- Did the form used to create the new user display any warnings, alerting that something went wrong?
- Did the form clear itself off of the information that was entered or did it just "sit there"?

Be that as it may, assuming that a Developer has fixed this issue and it now sits on your queue for verification, if you fail it by only writing a comment stating that "it doesn't work," you're just contributing to the problem!

I'm sure you can already hear the Developer asking you:

"Did you try the steps described in the original report?"

"Of course I did," you'll say. "I'm a Quality Engineer; I know what I'm doing!"

I'm sure that you, as a Quality Engineer followed the steps mentioned in the report and even did a bit more than that, but how is anyone other than yourself to know that? And depending on how this conversation took place, via emails or comments on the report itself, how much time has already been spent here with no valuable progress made other than perhaps getting people a bit cranky?

I realize that I may be exaggerating things a little bit here, but is it too far-fetched? I've seen it happen many times and I can tell you that this type of attitude is not only detrimental to the Team's morale, but also an impediment to the process of getting a much-needed resolution to the paying customers. Here's what I would have done if I were the person working on this:

First and foremost, if the application I'm testing logs errors and warnings to a log file in the filesystem, I would immediately watch its content and observe it for any useful information. Sounds like an obvious thing to do, doesn't? You'd be surprised how many people don't do it though. On a Linux-based operating system, the command *tail -f /var/log/<APPLICATION_NAME>/<SOME_FILE>.log* is your best friend! You can even follow multiple log files at the same time using the same command:

```
tail -f
/var/log/{<APPLICATION1_NAME>,<APPLICATION2_NA
ME>,<APPLICATION3_NAME>}/*.log
```

The command above would then help you keep an eye on what's being recorded on any log files (that's what the *.log means) found under the path /var/log for APPLICATION1, APPLICATION2, and APPLICATION3.

Now that I have them being watched closely, preferably on a separate window that is both close to the application and easily visible, I can proceed to the actual reproducing steps.

Open the Users page

1. Click the add button
2. Use Søren Jensen for name
3. Use sjensen for email
4. Click the save button

Based on the original issue, when the Save button was clicked at the end, nothing visually happened to indicate to the end user that something had failed. In my opinion, this in itself is worthy of a Usability defect report! If something internally has failed and prevented the expected outcome (adding a new user to the application), wouldn't it be better if some warning or error message was presented to the end user? Even if this last step had worked, wouldn't it be more user-friendly if a confirmation message was displayed stating that the new user was successfully created?

As a Quality Engineer, I believe a new defect report should be created providing contextual, clear information about the outcome of the action just performed. It reassures the end user that the application is working as expected. For the times when something does go wrong, it should make that fact known as well, leaving no room for ambiguity.

Some people may feel inclined to mark the current issue as having failed the verification process, but I disagree with this approach. I believe that the lack of a notification mechanism is entirely unrelated to the functionality being tested, i.e., user creation, and therefore a wholly new report should be filed.

Back to our example, after clicking on the Save button and noticing that indeed, nothing seems to happen and the new user is not created in the application, my next step would be to check the log files for anything useful. Were there any error or warning messages added to them when you clicked the button? Most of the time what you're looking for are errors and their corresponding stack traces, as they will contain a great deal of information from the application (or the operating system) which may be useful to a Developer, or even yourself.

If no errors or useful warning messages were displayed, and especially if we're testing a web application, how about checking for javascript error messages? Most if not all modern web browsers today offer the functionality of letting you inspect for these types of errors and even detect if anything is being sent (POST) or received (GET) from the application.

Furnished with this information, it is now acceptable to fail the verification of the issue, but remember that adding an "It doesn't work" message is not enough. What you want to do is to include as much information as possible so that whoever reads your comments has a clear picture as to what you did while testing the provided fix.

How do you do this? Write better defect reports and use positive, constructive words when doing so. It may sound funny, but if you want to have a good relationship with those who will fix the issue, watch your attitude and language!

Next, be specific! Include as much relevant information as possible:

- Did you follow the same steps provided in the report or did you deviate from it?
- If you deviated from the provided steps, what exactly did you do?
- What values did you enter into the application?
- What version of the product did you use? Remember that a Developer may be already working on the next version of your product, so this information would be useful to determine what code base to check.
- What operating system were you using?
- Were you using a web browser? If so, which one?
- Did you use a custom script or application during your testing? If you did, include it with instructions on how to use it.

If the problem manifests itself via the User Interface, include as many screenshots as needed to convey your point. Don't know how to explain it or don't think that a screenshot is doing the job? Record a short video and attach it to the report. Remember, the more information you can provide, the higher the chance the Developer reading your comments will understand what you're seeing.

Lastly, and I can't emphasize this enough, always include logs, especially if you think you saw something peculiar in them. If you're accessing logs that live on a remote server, you'll have to be comfortable transferring files between systems, perhaps even having to compress them before doing so. If you're not familiar with how to do this, I suggest you invest the time to learn more about the commands **SCP**, **rsync**, **tar**, and **zip**, to name a few.

Now that you have rejected the proposed solution for the defect, including as much information as you could gather, is it okay to finally consider your job done?

Quite the opposite my friend. Some people may be ready to tackle the next challenge, but it is my opinion that if you want to go beyond the expectations for a Quality Engineer, there are a few more things that you can do.

If a couple of days have passed and you haven't heard any news about the issue you failed, you can follow it up with the Developer! Check in with him or her and ask if more information is needed or if there is anything that you can do to help out. Some people may feel more comfortable with sending an email or adding a comment to the report, but If you're in the same building, I highly recommend that you walk down to the Developer's desk and have a friendly chat. We're all multitasking, whether we want to or not, and there could be a myriad of reasons for the lack of updates on your defect.

For example, since a Developer will most likely be using a personal laptop to write their code, they may not necessarily have access to a larger, more robust server that resembles what the customer uses. They may also not yet have a more holistic understanding of how the application works under a "real world" environment, and therefore may not be in a position to create it to test their solution.

So if during your chat you learn that they don't have a system that lets them easily reproduce the required setting, or that they don't have a tool or automated process to populate the application with the proper dataset, give it to them! Chances are, and I certainly hope so, that as a Quality Engineer, you will have significant, enterprise-like servers with large swaths of disk space and RAM to ensure that you're testing the product exactly as the customer would. I'd also posit that you have an automated test or script that can be used to configure the system exactly as is needed to reproduce the defect (and if you don't, you should!).

The point is, reach out across the proverbial aisle and help them overcome their obstacles. We all want what is best for our customers, right? If we all work together and collaborate, we all win!

Lastly, remember when I mentioned in an earlier chapter that there is a stereotype that Quality Engineers don't write code? Well, I want to say that as you become more and more accustomed to testing the product, I'm sure that you'll come across numerous opportunities to see the source code that makes up the application. There is no doubt in my mind that it is only a matter of time until someone in Quality Engineering starts looking "under the hood" and correlating the code changes introduced by the Developers to the files installed on their systems. Do this often enough, and you start seeing patterns and learning about which files do what.

Then, one day, you may find yourself in the unique position of not only filing a new defect against the product but of also providing the code change (i.e., patch) that fixes the issue! Since all of our products at Red Hat are open sourced, anyone, including the Quality Engineers, has access to their source code. Whenever one of our Engineers get to a point in their career when they start submitting patches with their defect reports, I consider it a rite of passage for them! It is then that, in my opinion, you stop just "doing your job" and truly become part of the solution!

It is only when the customer receives an acceptable fix for the defect that they reported that a Quality Engineer could consider their part done!

Ain't Nobody Got Time For That

Assuming that you're well on your way of mastery in becoming a Quality Engineer, your day to day activities could start looking a little bit out of control. You could find yourself attending your feature teams scrum meetings, reviewing automation results from nightly test suites, following up with development teams about fixes for the defects you care about, checking on the latest code commits, all the while keeping an eye on the incoming major release. The list of activities could go on and on depending on what level of interaction and collaboration at which you find yourself.

It is the point where veteran Quality Engineers may start questioning their sanity for choosing such a crazy and chaotic career path, and newly inducted aspiring Testers tend to curl up into a fetal position, wondering if they will ever survive until the end of the week without having a panic attack! It is also another essential rite of passage which will determine whether you can take the next step in your career or if you've reached the end of the road.

Through the years I have gone through this rite of passage a few times, each one of them setting the point at which my career took off and led me to yet another new exciting chapter! It was just when all of my successes and accomplishments seemed to be about to unravel, and my mental and physical stability were one extra task away from a total breakdown that I was able to see a new path out of the impending madness and found myself rising to a new level in my career. Coincidentally, these moments were also followed by salary increases, promotions, or both!

You may be thinking that I'm either exaggerating things, making up stories, or just full of crap, and while I won't tell you which one of them is correct, I will tell you what my secret move was instead. What follows is one of my secret keys to success in this crazy world of software testing. I cannot claim that it will apply to your specific case or if it will increase your chances of success and career growth, but I am 100% certain that it worked exceptionally well for me! As the old saying goes, your mileage may (and will) vary, and I can only hope that it will be helpful to you as well, or at least help you keep your sanity intact.

The secret is quite simple: you cannot do everything at the same time, all the time! There! Simple, isn't it? I'm sure that I am not telling you anything new and that you're probably wondering if you should continue reading this chapter, let alone finish the remainder of the book. But answer me this: if it is so obvious and straightforward, why aren't you using it to wrangle your tasks and schedule into submission, huh? Executing simple solutions well may not be as apparent as you may think, and I hope you'll find the way I did it inspiring or at least somewhat helpful.

The first thing I do when I come across these situations, and as I pointed out, they happen very often as your career progresses, is list all the key responsibilities and tasks for my current role. Some folks may like to take notes on text editors or some note-taking application, but I prefer to keep things simple and use paper and pen or pencil, whichever is handy.

As a Senior Quality Engineer working on the Red Hat Satellite product, for example, my list could look a lot like the following:

- Review automation results and failures from our nightly automated builds
- Attend in person or dial-in to our daily team scrum calls
- Fix failures from nightly builds, if any (which could happen a lot with some types of system or integration-level tests)

- Verify that a delivered code fix from our development team does indeed resolve the reported defect by executing a series of actions to validate their changes
- Help a developer test their in-flight code fix by patching a deployed system with their changes before the code gets merged into the main source code branch
- Write user stories or test cases and review them with developers and product manager for new features during the planning phase
- Put out the many fires that come with the territory, including dealing with out-of-band hotfixes for existing customers or minor emergency releases due to third-party dependencies getting out of sync

Just reliving these scenarios right now makes my head spin! How you keep track of so many tasks and handle them with a high level of performance is something that can only be described as "being in the zone," that moment where you're moving on auto-pilot and minutes blur into hours which blur into days and releases get shipped on time without you noticing. As glamorous as it may sound to be able to do all of these things without realizing, there is only so much one can do before your health and personal life starts to be affected.

So now that you have your list in front of you, the next step is to categorize them in the order of their priority, dependency, and return on investment (ROI).

Tasks that are of high priority should get addressed as early as possible on your schedule. While it is easy to say or think that every job is a priority for you, if you take a more in-depth look, you may find that some are more important than others. It is crucial that you develop the appropriate skills and knowledge to quickly identify which ones must get done come hell or high water! If these things don't get done, nothing else matters!

Once the critical path is cleared, you may **not** want to immediately jump to the next high-severity task on your list. Why not? I think that it will depend on how much time you may have left to complete them, how stressful your day has been so far, or if you have all the information you need to finish them. Sometimes, the best reason could be that you need a break! I lost count of how many times I was able to knock out what looked like a hairy and complicated task in less than 10 minutes just because I decided to wait for a few hours or even the next day to work on it.

Lastly, you have those tasks that if you were only to invest some time to handle them, they might never become a task again, ever! These are the things that are not necessarily complicated and could be quickly done with a basic shell or

Python script, but you just never took the time to do it. Sure you could continue to do them manually or even manually run the script, assuming you took the time to write it, but it is something that requires a context switch and throws you off your schedule or rhythm.

Now, I know that there is no such thing as a free lunch, and if you stop to write that script or add it to an automated process that can be easily triggered whenever needed, it will take you away from all the high priority tasks which you're supposed to be working. If you're like me, then you'll probably eventually get bored or upset for wasting your time doing something repetitive, and that represents an interruption into an already chaotic schedule. The time you invest in turning these important but annoying types of tasks may look like a high price to pay, but trust me that the sooner you pay this price, the sooner you'll be able to enjoy the dividends of having a reliable, automated way for dealing with them!

This final list may still look daunting to you, but the next step should help alleviate your fears: add them to your weekly calendar, making sure to scope the date and time in which you intend to get them completed. Easier said than done? Well, take a look at the following example:

	Monday	Tuesday	Wednesday	Thursday	Friday
09:00 - 10:00	Review Auto	Review Auto	Review Auto	Review Auto	Review Auto
10:00 - 11:00	Scrum	Scrum	Scrum	Scrum	Scrum
11:00 - 12:00	Feature	Feature	Feature	Feature	Feature
12:00 - 13:00	Lunch	Lunch	Lunch	Lunch	Lunch
13:00 - 14:00	Personal	Personal	Personal	Personal	Personal

14:00 - 15:00	Fix Failures	Automation	Automation	Automation	Automation
15:00 - 16:00	Fix Failures	Automation	Automation	Automation	Automation
16:00 - 17:00	Fix Failures	Automation	Automation	Automation	Automation

I understand that this may look like an oversimplified schedule, or it may look like every single minute of your days are accounted for, but my point is that you can and should take ownership of your time and wisely choose where you want to spend your time!

For this specific scenario, let us assume that a brand new feature has just started going through the initial planning and design phase. Based on my experience working on situations like this one, the first or even the second week of planning won't require a whole lot of your time. I could, however, reserve one full hour to attend daily scrums followed by another entire hour to review any existing documentation, have productive discussions with the feature team, or even do some research on the subject, if it is something new to you. Do you need one whole hour for a scrum? Do most feature teams meet every day? Not necessarily, but the point is that you can find the time to deal with it.

Also observe that I have reserved one hour for lunch, something that may look strange to you, but when things get out of hand, you may find yourself joining meetings or working through the time when you're supposed to be relaxing and recharging your batteries. Furthermore, I could choose to spend an additional hour, which I called Personal Time, to either socialize, rest, or read up on the latest news or technologies to make sure that I invest in my personal growth.

The rest of the time is carved out for reviewing nightly automation results and either fixing whatever needs to be fixed or adding new automated tests to your test suite.

Let's fast-forward a few weeks, and the scenario now includes multiple things happening at the same time: your feature is mature enough that you can start to automate your test cases, while you're also helping out with the verification of defects for an ongoing release. You're still supposed to review nightly builds and attend your scrums. Could you still manage to find time for yourself? Yes!

	Monday	Tuesday	Wednesday	Thursday	Friday
09:00 - 10:00	Review Auto	Review Auto	Review Auto	Review Auto	Review Auto
10:00 - 11:00	Fix Failures	Fix Failures	Automation	Automation	Automation
11:00 - 12:00	Scrum	Scrum	Scrum	Scrum	Scrum
12:00 - 13:00	Lunch	Lunch	Lunch	Lunch	Lunch
13:00 -	Personal	Personal	Personal	Personal	Personal

14:00					
14:00 - 15:00	Verify Bug	Verify Bug	Verify Bug	Verify Bug	Verify Bug
15:00 - 16:00	Automati on	Automati on	Automati on	Automati on	Automati on
16:00 - 17:00	Automati on	Automati on	Automati on	Automati on	Automati on

Once again, I have identified my priorities, the order that I want or need to work on them, followed by a carefully crafted schedule that not only allows me to find time to rest and invest in myself but also doesn't force me to work crazy hours!

It may take a few iterations to get the right schedule that works best for you (I, for example, prefer to carve out some "me" time on Friday afternoons), so feel free to experiment and move around the things you have control over. Once you do find the right combination, try your best to stick to it, and if anything new arrives for you to work on, move it to its specific time slot, according to its priority, dependency, and ROI.

Eventually, there may come a day when your schedule won't allow you to add anything else unless you extend your day by a couple of hours or drop something else in favor of the new thing. It is a pretty crucial decision that you'll have to make: should you add a few extra hours to your jam-packed schedule or do you tell your manager that one of your existing tasks will have to move to your backlog of activities and get addressed at a later time?

Please keep in mind that the answer to this question carries a lot of consequences, both for the short and long term of your career: adding something to a backlog creates a technical debt, and sooner or later you'll have to get to it. You're just postponing it, and as long as you don't make this a permanent "solution" to this type of situation, for most of the time, you should be able to "pay" this debt shortly after you complete the new task. If you don't, however, you'll run the risk of creating an ever-growing, never-ending list of chores to finish, and the chances are that you might end up carrying it for a very long time.

My advice: avoid, as much as possible, creating a technical debt! Talk to your manager about the prioritization for any new jobs that come your way, and figure out if something else can be removed from your schedule or moved to someone else. If something ends up going into your backlog, discuss the timing for when you can go back to it, and this way pay it off as soon as possible!

If you decide to extend your schedule and work a couple of extra hours, please keep in mind that while you may feel up to the challenge, it is just as crucial for your career to find the right work-to-personal-life balance! While I believe that most managers will appreciate and acknowledge anyone for putting the extra time to get the project moving forward or for helping through a critical situation, you have to find the time to "recharge your batteries," and invest in socializing with your family, friends, and peers. It is especially true for those out there who have a family, life partner or someone special in their lives, and I would like to talk about this topic next.

The Balancing Act

One of the benefits I most enjoyed when I switched to working for a software startup company back in 2006 was the flexibility I had with my schedule. Whereas before as a consultant in the New York City area I had to track my hours carefully and clock-in and clock-out every time I entered or left the office, people at my new job could not care less about it!

I understand that consultants get paid by the hour, and therefore it is essential to track hours worked so that people get paid what they're owed, but even before I worked as a consultant I felt that I was expected to be at work and be productive from 08:00 to 17:00, all the time! It was as if writing code is something you turn on and off at will, and that faucet was supposed to be on 8 hours a day, seven days a week!

When I joined rPath in 2006, I learned first from my then manager that my value was not measured only by the number of lines of code I cranked out every day. The way I worked out the problems I faced and the way I collaborated and innovated with my teammates was much more important! People's potential was carefully nurtured and given proper training and time to develop and bloom at their own pace! Our performance was not something measured by how many hours we were at the office.

Some people may think that this "lack" of structure could only lead to employee abuse or low productivity, but the truth was that we all wanted to be the best that we could be! Day in, day out, we all managed to complete our tasks mostly on time, and it didn't require anyone to be typing at their keyboard all the time. I like to think that the flexibility and trust they placed in us played a significant role in our success! It was both refreshing and empowering to be treated like a professional and trusted that I was working as hard as I could, even when I was not banging at my keyboard.

Part of this new flexibility included being able to take a few hours here or there to take care of myself or my family, attending my kids' school events (prior to rPath I had missed many of those), taking a more extended lunch to meet with friends, or even taking a "sanity" day off to relax and focus on myself! I found this freedom intoxicating.

Being a responsible person and professional, I never allowed myself to take advantage of this system, and so I worked all the time to make sure that I was earning my paycheck, being a valuable team member, with a few extra hours thrown in to help with the steep learning curve I faced when I first joined. This work ethic is something I am very proud of, and something that I brought with me when I joined Red Hat in 2011.

To this day I still hear from some of my closest teammates how they can't figure out how I can keep up with so many emails, chat conversations, discussions and new features while being a father of 3 young kids, maintaining a marriage of almost 19 years, and finding time to read an average of 70 books a year. "How do you do that?" they ask me.

My "formula" took a while to develop, and it required many iterations and lessons learned the hard way. If you walked into my home-office about 7 years ago, you would have found me sitting in front of 4 23-inch monitors, two computers and multiple applications running at the same time. I had a monitor entirely dedicated to IRC chat windows from 4 different servers, another one for email (personal and work), and two other monitors to write code and test things. A laptop sat to my right so that I could see what was happening on Twitter. I wanted information all the time, and even when I was not in front of the computer, my IRC sessions were logging everything for me so that I could catch up on everything I had missed overnight. For many years, this was my modus operandi.

As my kids grew older, however, I realized that if I wanted to have more time for my family and myself, something would have to change. My working hours were taking over my life, and I would have to be a bit more selective as to what type of information was still important and necessary for me to continue doing my job well, both as a Red Hatter but also as a doting father and husband.

I started by taking baby steps, turning off my chat windows when I clocked out for the day. Granted I worked until 18:00 most days, but once I was done for the day, nothing was luring me back to my home office. The world would have to wait for me until I signed back in the next day. I also switched from a text-based IRC client (irssi running on a screen session) to something with a graphical interface that would alert me if anyone had sent me a direct message or mentioned my name. I also kept this new application minimized at all times so that I would not get distracted during the day with other conversations not immediately related to what I was supposed to be working on.

The next step was to choose which channels I still cared about and were essential to my job and interests, which brought me down to a total of about eight from approximately fifty channels originally.

The second item I addressed was to unsubscribe from mailing lists that no longer were important to me, and through the years I had been subscribed to several dozen lists! The criteria I used was basically to identify which lists I had started filtering out into their inboxes and that I had ignored for more than one month. This process took me a while because there were always some lists which I tried to convince myself that I would eventually get to, but deep down I knew that I never really would.

Getting rid of about 85% of my mailing lists brought my daily influx of emails from a few thousand emails to a more manageable few hundred, but I still cringed every morning when I would log in for the day and see that massive pile waiting for me. It got to a point where even taking a sick day, or vacation was something I was reluctant to do since a couple of days without checking emails could translate into spending an entire day just trying to catch up, weeding out what needed to be addressed from what was just noise.

Going through some of my email exchange with developers I noticed an interesting pattern: no matter what time I send them an email, I would only hear back from them either in the afternoon or early the next morning. It was almost like they never made a point of checking their email all the time like I was. Could it be that the world would not end if you didn't reply to an email within minutes of reading it? I thought that perhaps they were onto something here.

I gave the "check email early and late afternoon" a trial of a couple of weeks, but that still was not helping me with the sheer number of emails I was receiving. I confess that while not having my email open all the time was supposed to allow

137

me to focus on other things, I kept thinking about the fact that once I did check it, I would still face the daunting task of parsing through hundreds of messages to see what really required my attention. After those first two weeks, I was back to keeping my email client open all the time!

Then, one day, I came across an interesting article that offered a different method to get your inbox under control. It proposed such a simple trick, and many useful tricks are apparently, that I'm surprised that I didn't flat out ignore it right away. I guess I was getting close to losing hope, the point where you're willing to try just about anything because you have nothing to lose. So I did.

First, I created a filter that redirected any email where the "To" or "CC" fields contained my email, which eliminated anything that arrived from a mailing list. These emails were redirected into a Priority folder and became the main focus area for my email browsing activities. This simple filter cut down the number of things I needed to address by about a third of my daily total.

From my Priority folder, I then proceeded to further filter things out by redirecting emails into folders carefully labeled starting with a number, followed by a hyphen and the name of the person who had sent it. I chose to use zero for my highest priority emails, reserved for my manager and my direct reports, and one for anyone else. For example:

- 0-Boss
- 0-Joe (direct report)
- 0-Mary (direct report)
- 1-Beth (reports to Joe)
- 1-Mario (reports to Mary)

Anything else that did not fall into this categorization was left on my Priority folder, and I could then figure out what to do with it. After a while, I could decide whether I wanted to keep those emails prioritized or if I should find a way to stop them from arriving (which turned out to be spam from services I had once subscribed to at some time in the past.)

Now, when I check my emails, I usually have less than 100 for the entire day to go through, but only 30 of them requiring a direct reply from me. I start with my zero-priority emails first, followed by the ones and even if I decide to keep my email client open all the time, there is nothing that prevents me from completely ignoring it for most of the day.

Another advantage of this system is that I can quickly check my email from my phone before going to sleep. I can see if anything requires my prompt reply (which happens when you have people reporting to you from multiple timezones) or at least be aware of something that will need my attention when I log in the next day.

I honestly can say that I feel much freer than I was about one year ago and am no longer a slave to my inbox or chat channels. I have since then switched to using Slack and Google Chat, which I either keep minimized or don't open at all unless I get notified on my phone that someone has sent me a message. I can then decide whether I need to reply right away or if it is something I can postpone until I am ready for it. I have also stopped looking at Twitter and closed my Facebook accounts, which saves me from numerous interruptions during the day!

I like to think that I now have a steady career and personal lifestyle. When I'm working, I'm more focused than ever and wholly dedicated to my job and the people I work with. In the same token, when I clock out, I'm fully committed to my family and myself. I continue to read many books every year and even found time to swim a few laps in the pool during the week. My wife and I have lunch together every day (I work from home), we both pick up our youngest daughter from pre-K every afternoon and have dinner with our three daughters every night. I wouldn't have it any other way for anything in the world!

Acknowledgements

This book would not be possible if it weren't for my mother, **Elza Maciel**. Having been born with a rare congenital disease in a country like Brazil in the early 1970s, my 24-year-old mother decided that my life would not be dictated by my physical disability or by what doctors told her my life expectancy would be. Armed with a tremendous determination to seek treatment for my condition, she quite literally carried me all over the country, many times with no money or food or a place to stay, never giving up hope for a better life for me. To her, I owe it all, and there is absolutely nobody else in the known and unknown universe that has single-handedly shaped and positively influenced me as much as she has!

I also owe a massive debt of gratitude to the relentless, unwavering and unconditional support of my lovely wife, **Elizabeth**. Managing a house full of young kids, a newly adopted 11-year-old dog, and a husband who works from home, consuming absurd amounts of coffee and who decided to spend whatever free time he had to write a book, means that she is all over the place and never rests. I'm forever in awe at how she just brushes things off and is, day in, day out, a loving, caring, understanding and forgiving partner in crime!

To **Vinny DaSilva** who a few years ago, while visiting from Massachusetts, unintentionally helped me see my own defects and completely turn my career around at a pivotal moment of my professional life. I can honestly say that I either would not be where I am today (or perhaps it would have taken me much longer to get here) if it wasn't for that one day I went out with Vinny to grab a cup of coffee and forced him to listen to me whine about my life and career choices. This was the turning point!

To **Andrew McCabe**, to whom I owe many hours of mentoring and teachings in the field of Quality Engineering and without whom I would not be doing (and loving) what I do today! Andy was and continues to be a role model to me, and no matter what I end up doing in the future or how many different roles I may ever take, I will forever be indebted to him.

To my former manager **Edward Bailey**, who gave me a life-changing second chance, when he could have easily let me go, and for teaching me that "investing" on people is the best type of investment one can make in life.

To my former manager **Chandrasekar Kannan**, who taught me how to take all of my passion and energy, manage and channel them into a more diplomatic message.

To my current manager **Shai Revivo**, who:

- Taught me the always come prepared with a second proposal whenever dealing with crucial conversations
- Instilled in me the desire to be a more data-driven manager
- Pushed me the hardest in my life (second only to my mother) by never letting me get too comfortable at work
- One day many years ago, standing atop a mountain of snow somewhere in Europe while on vacation so to get a better cellphone signal, talked me into not leaving Red Hat because he believed in my talent and dream of creating the next generation of Quality Engineers at work.

Despite my (many) mistakes and blunders early in my career, these three people saw the hidden potential and provided me with the time, space and opportunities to learn and grow.

To **Dan Bader**, who provided me with valuable information and ideas about how this book should be formatted and provided me with genuine interest and support for what I wanted to write about.

To **Jon Allen** who offered to go through my book checking for typos, mistakes, and provided great editing suggestions.

To my longtime friends, **Evandro Pastor** and **Peter Savage** for being a never exhausting source of support, inspiration, and accepting to jump in into whatever crazy ideas I cook up, never questioning my intentions, never wavering in their unconditional friendship, and always committed to helping me, no matter what!

About The Author

Og B. Maciel has over ten years of experience working in different roles as a Quality Engineer and is currently Director of Quality Engineering and proud to work with a diverse and extensive team of Quality Engineers at Red Hat.

He lives in the outskirts of Chapel Hill, North Carolina, with his wife, three daughters and Lucky, their adopted golden retriever.